Buddhist Emptiness and Christian Trinity

ESSAYS AND EXPLORATIONS

edited by
Roger Corless
and
Paul F. Knitter

PAULIST PRESS
New York/Mahwah, N.J.

ACKNOWLEDGMENT:
Excerpts from *Does God Exist?* by Hans Küng. Copyright © 1978, 1979, 1980 by Double-day, a division of Bantam Doubleday Dell Publishing Group, Inc. Reprinted by permission of the publisher.

Library of Congress Cataloging-in-Publication Data

Buddhist emptiness and Christian trinity: essays and explorations/edited by Roger Corless
and Paul F. Knitter.
    p. cm.
    Includes bibliographical references.
    ISBN 0-8091-3131-5
    1. Christianity and other religions—Buddhism. 2. Buddhism—Relations—Chris-tianity. 3. Shūnyatā. 4. Trinity. I. Corless, Roger. II. Knitter, Paul F.
BR128.B8B834   1990
231—dc20   89-38420
                                  CIP

Published by Paulist Press
997 Macarthur Boulevard
Mahwah, New Jersey 07430

Printed and bound in the
United States of America

Contents

Introduction 1
    Roger Corless

Kenosis and Emptiness 5
    Masao Abe

God's Self-Renunciation and Buddhist Emptiness:
A Christian Response to Masao Abe 26
    Hans Küng

Buddhist Shūnyatā and the Christian Trinity:
The Emerging Holistic Paradigm 44
    Michael von Brück

Buddhist Shūnyatā and the Christian Trinity:
A Response to Michael von Brück 67
    Paul O. Ingram

Can Emptiness Will? 75
    Roger Gregory-Tashi Corless

Can Will Be Predicated of Emptiness?
A Response to Roger Corless 97
    Durwood Foster

Bibliographical References 103

Notes on the Contributors 108

Introduction

Roger Corless

*T*his volume presents some high level musings about two elements in Buddhism and Christianity which control their respective systems. As a way of grabbing the reader's attention, I could say that these essays speak about God and the Buddha. But, in fact, they do not. Or, not quite.

The question "Is the Buddha like God?" demands to be asked, and no matter how often I try to crush it, not only in my students but also in myself, I find it springing up again. However, we really do not, at this early stage in the developing discipline of Buddhist-Christian studies, know what the question means, or even how to ask it meaningfully. The Buddhas and the Christian God function in their own universes and it is not at all clear whether these universes relate to each other at all, and, if they do, in what way or ways. We need to go behind the question "Is the Buddha (or, are the Buddhas) like God?" and uncover the question, or questions, which led up to it.

These essays try to do this. They are exploratory and tentative, confusing, and even (speaking as much for myself as for my fellow contributors) confused. When I reread what I have written, I find that I am not sure that I know what I am trying to say, and as I was editing the essays of my distinguished colleagues, I sometimes wondered if they might not have similar reactions to their own work. We are pushing into unexplored territory, and cutting a path as we go. If it turns out that, unfortunately, we have cut the wrong one, others will be able to recognize this because of our labors in opening up the *terra incognita.* But we hope, of course, that we are moving in the right direction.

This book, then, is a series of questions. Each essay is followed by a learned response which raises more questions, and it was our collective

1

decision not to respond to the responses, but to leave the essays and responses in a somewhat raw, open state, allowing the reader to enter into our dialogue and be stimulated to his or her own reflections.

Each author examines the Christian God (clearly understood as the Triune God of Christian experience rather than the "One" of the philosophers so roundly and correctly criticized by Pascal) and the Emptiness (*shūnyatā*) of Mahayana Buddhism's understanding of Reality. They then look for comparisons, contrasts, and "resonances" (von Brück's word) between such a God and such a Reality.

Masao Abe challenges the viewpoint that God is a Something while Emptiness is a Nothing by, first of all, examining God and Emptiness with some sophistication, and then proposing (perhaps a little mischievously) the reverse: that God is empty and Emptiness is full. In his response, Hans Küng both builds upon this and criticizes it for being incompletely Trinitarian.

Michael von Brück presents us with the Buddhist Emptiness, the Christian Trinity, and the physicist David Bohm's holographic hypothesis, as mutually resonant symbols of that cosmic wholeness which the modern world is seeking. His paper is a series of dense and powerful images, and it demands much of the reader, but those who work with it carefully will find that they have been given a new vision. Paul Ingram responds with appreciation for this vision, but finds that von Brück's arguments bristle with philosophical difficulties.

In my own paper, I likewise work with images, beginning with a dream or, as I might better say, a myth, were it not so easy to misunderstand that word as meaning fiction. Truthfully, I would like to have ended there, for I feel that the myth which showed itself to me is what the Dharma and the Gospel really wanted to say through me, and having said it, I am done. But I am a professor, and so I go on and try to explain myself. I have attempted to expand on my proposal of the co-inherence of Buddhism and Christianity (Corless, 1986) by seeing it in the light of David Bohm's holographic hypothesis, which I find to be a useful allegory (my use of it being, I think, "softer" than von Brück would like) for putting the co-inherence into motion. But, as Durwood Foster remarks, I am more provocative than I am clear.

All three essays in this volume were originally presented as papers at a conference which sought to examine Buddhism and Christianity in terms of Thomas Kuhn's hermeneutic of "paradigm shift" (Kuhn, 1970), called "Paradigm Shifts in Buddhism and Christianity: Cultural Systems

Introduction 3

and the Self," held at Hawaii Loa College, Windward O'ahu, Hawaii, January 3–11, 1984. The essays formed part of a panel on Theological Encounter on the morning of Thursday, January 5, chaired by Paul Knitter of Xavier University in Cincinnati. To the surprise and delight of the participants, each paper was found (by the providence of God and/or an auspicious karmic conjunction) to be part of a unified presentation, and it was decided to publish them as a unit. Written responses were solicited to the papers after they had been revised by their authors.

Kenosis and Emptiness

Masao Abe

*T*he dialogue between Buddhism and Christianity has evolved considerably over the past few decades. The dialogue no longer remains merely at the stage of promoting mutual understanding between the two religions. Going a step further, the dialogue is entering a new stage in which the mutual transformation of Buddhism and Christianity is seriously being explored.[1] This new development is taking place not only in terms of theology or doctrinal understanding, but also in the field of practical spirituality. This tendency, I hope, will continue to accelerate in the future.

The dialogue between Buddhism and Christianity, however, should not be regarded simply as an interfaith dialogue. It must be undertaken also with an awareness of a wider socio-cultural-historical dimension, while it presupposes the existence and significance of religion. Many people in our secularized society ask, "Why is religion necessary?" and "What meaning does religion have for us today?" They think they can well live without religion and thus are quite skeptical about or indifferent toward religion. Furthermore, ideologies which negate religion, such as Scientism, Marxism, Freudianism, and Nihilism in the Nietzschian sense, prevail in our society. All of these ideologies deny the *raison d'être* of religion, not merely on emotional grounds but, equally, though from different angles, on rational or theoretical grounds. Far beyond criticism of a particular religion such as Buddhism or Christianity, these ideologies now direct scathing criticism against the very being of religion itself. The most basic issue for any religion in our time, therefore, is to be responsive to these anti-religious forces by elucidating the authentic meaning of religious faith. This is the reason why, as early as 1963, in a paper entitled "Buddhism and Christianity as a Problem of Today," I emphasized:

5

Self-estrangement - most serious question
Search for a new Paradigm

MASAO ABE

Apart from the context of the issue between religion and irreligion there wouldn't be much sense in taking up the problem of Buddhism and Christianity. If a discussion of the theme should not throw any light on our search for the being of religion itself which can overpower all negation, then it would be indeed futile to engage in it. It is precisely at the meeting point of the two problems, namely the interreligious problem of Buddhism and Christianity on the one hand, and the problem of religion and irreligion on the other, that the most serious question for modern man, the question of his self-estrangement should be asked: and it is precisely there that we may expect to find an answer to it (Abe, 1963).

The necessity of tackling the Buddhist-Christian dialogue not merely in terms of interfaith dialogue, but also as an inseparable part of the wider, socio-cultural problem of religion versus irreligion has become more and more pressing in the past few decades. To use the terminology of Thomas S. Kuhn and Hans Küng, both Buddhism and Christianity are now facing "a transitional period of uncertainty" or "crisis" in which the continuous "organic development," or the usual cumulative process of "normal science," is no longer appropriate (Kuhn, 1970: 66–76; Küng, n.d.: 7–8). It is an urgent task for both religions to pursue a fundamental reorganization in characterizing their faith such that the prevailing basic assumptions are drastically changed—for example, a revolutionary reinterpretation of the concept of God in Christianity and the concept of Emptiness in Buddhism—thereby allowing a new paradigm or model of understanding to emerge. Insofar as Buddhist-Christian dialogue is undertaken merely as an interfaith dialogue which takes religion's existence and significance for granted it does not penetrate to the core of the present crisis which all religions are facing, and it will not lead to the much-needed search for a new paradigm.

In this paper I will confine my discussion to Scientism and Nietzschian Nihilism.

Scientism

We should not confuse the basis on which science stands with the basis on which Scientism stands. The standpoint of science does not necessarily contradict that of religion. Of course these two approaches, science and religion, have some points of essential difference, but they do

Scientism claims that science is absolute truth [handwritten annotation]

not always mutually exclude one another, and are at least potentially compatible. The standpoint of Scientism, however, can never be compatible with that of religion, for Scientism, by making the standpoint of science absolute, claims the scientific method to be the one and only criterion of truth. Anything nonscientific becomes false. Thus, religion, being nonscientific, is considered false according to Scientistic thinking. Since science has made remarkable advances in modern times, and since scientific laws are subject to widely accepted forms of experimental demonstration, scientific truth has impressed many people as the absolute truth, although it is only one kind of truth. While eminent scientists rarely espouse Scientism, there are, however, many nonscientists and scientists who judge everything in a Scientistic way. If the scientific truth is taken as the only criterion of truth, the dismissal of religion inevitably follows. Proponents of Scientism maintain that religion still exists today only because the scientific way of thinking has not yet sufficiently permeated the masses. Scientism believes that religion will naturally cease to exist once science has progressed to the extent that the scientific way of thinking is embraced by all. For Scientism, the continued existence of religion has nothing to do with the nature or essence of religion, but merely reflects some slowness in its inevitable demise. Religion is dismissed in principle by Scientism.

The question of what scientific method is, is important. Classical physics was based on mathematical rationality and viewed humans and nature mechanistically. In contrast to this older view, contemporary physics, with the theory of relativity (Einstein), and the uncertainty principle (Heisenberg), does not regard its method and the perceived truth as absolute. As Hans Küng expresses it:

Hence today, in physics, chemistry, biology and other natural sciences, it is customary to speak not of universally valid truths copying reality but of hypothetically valid "projects" and "patterns" that hold only in virtue of certain conditions and within certain limits, while fully permitting the coexistence of other projects and patterns.—An absolutely objective truth is not envisaged but only one that is relatively objective. In perspectivity and variability, any number of methods and aspects, projects and patterns, are possible in regard to the one reality, which itself always remains infinitely richer and more complex than all the statements—even the most exact—about it (Küng, 1980: 109f).

Scientism is a dogma ad an ideology
substituty belief in science for belief in God

8   MASAO ABE

In contemporary physics, the mechanistic and strictly objective view of nature in classical physics has been radically changed into a relativistic and more process-oriented view. As a result of this change, the implications of the term "scientific" are less mechanical and consequently less incompatible with religion than previously.

This does not mean, though, that contemporary science is no longer a challenge to religion. However relativistic the contemporary scientific view may be, if its perspective is dogmatized, or is taken ideologically, it turns into a form of Scientism. In this regard, I agree with Hans Küng when he says: "The idea of critical rationality must be entirely approved; but the ideology of a critical rationalism, absolutizing and mysticizing the rational factor, must be rejected.—Rationalistic ideology is characterized by rationalistic dogmatism and rationalistic intolerance" (Küng, 1980: 124).

Hans Küng also reminds us that in the sixteenth and seventeenth centuries, because of its failure to become allies with the new science and the new philosophical and social-political developments, the Church contributed substantially to the rise of both scientific and political atheism. But Küng insists: "There was, however, no necessity in principle for autonomous reason, for modern natural science, increasingly so to generalize their conclusion as to leave no place for a belief in God and in practice largely to substitute belief in science for belief in God" (Küng, 1980: 123f). While I have no real objection to this statement, I am tempted to ask how belief in God can embrace autonomous reason without marring it. It is clear that Küng emphasizes: "The God of the Bible is not identical with the God of the ancient world picture or with the God of Greek philosophy" (Küng, 1980: 124). God in the Bible is "one who faces me, whom I can address [and is] subject and not predicate: it is not that love is God, but that God is love" (Küng, 1980: 634). Precisely in this sense, God in the Bible is "a thou who may be called person and personal or even suprapersonal and transpersonal" (Küng, 1980: 634). If, as Küng rightly suggests, we must entirely approve the idea of critical rationality and autonomous reason, what is the ground on which critical rationality, autonomous reason, and God as Thou are not only compatible, but also work positively together without detracting from one another?

This challenge of modern science is serious for Christianity but much less serious for Buddhism because the basis of Buddhism is not faith in a God who faces us and can be addressed as a Thou, but it is the awakening to the Dharma (truth) which is termed Suchness or Emptiness. Even Pure Land Buddhism, which, like Christianity, emphasizes faith (in this case in Amida Buddha) takes Suchness or Emptiness as the basic Reality (Dharmakaya). Nevertheless, Buddhism must still address the issue of how the Buddhist notion of Suchness or Emptiness can embrace critical rationality while still allowing reason to function autonomously. An important task for contemporary Buddhist thinkers is to demonstrate the religious significance of Buddhist truth in relation to scientific truth.

Nihilism[2]

The problem of Nihilism *for us today* is not an emotional problem masquerading as an intellectual one, nor a recurrence of the age-old issue of nihilistic feeling often found in both East and West. Since the writings of Friedrich Nietzsche, Nihilism is no longer an emotional and timeless theme universally seen in human history, but has become an acute issue, which, through a sharp historical awareness of human destiny, demands of the modern person a radical rethinking of the foundations of cultural and religious life. Indeed, Nietzsche's Nihilism is an existential realization clearly based on a philosophy of history. This is, I think, why Heidegger says: "Nietzsche thinks of Nihilism and the 'inner logic' of occidental history" (Heidegger, 1950: 206, my translation). Elucidating Nietzsche's phrase 'God is dead,' Heidegger says: "The names of God and the Christian God in Nietzsche's thought are used as the designation for the supersensible world in general" (p. 199) and "the phrase 'God is dead' means: the supersensible world is without active power. It dispenses no life" (Heidegger, 1950: 200). Nietzsche's Nihilism is nothing but an acute realization, through the history of European nations, that "the highest values are 'depreciated' (*sich entwerten*) (Nietzsche, *Wille,* 1906: 10) entirely deprived of meaning." The highest values mean here the supersensible world established by Platonism as well as by Christianity.

In his book, *Beyond Good and Evil,* Nietzsche presents his unique idea of the three stages of human history:

> Once upon a time, men sacrificed human beings to their God, and perhaps just those they loved the best. Then, during the moral epoch of mankind, they sacrificed to their God the strongest instincts they possessed, their 'nature'; *this* festal joy shines in the cruel glances of ascetics and 'anti-natural' fanatics. Finally, what still remained to be sacrificed? Was it not necessary

to sacrifice God himself? To sacrifice God for nothingness—
this paradoxical mystery of the ultimate cruelty had been re-
served for the rising generation; we all know something of itself
already (Nietzsche, *Complete Works*, 12:73).

To the first stage of human history, Nietzsche ascribes the sacrifice of
all primitive religions and also the sacrifice of the Emperor Tiberius in the
Mithraeum on the island of Capri. It may be said that this first stage
corresponds to the time of the Old Testament which records the story of
this kind of sacrifice in the case, for example, of Abraham and Isaac. It
would also be safe to say that the second state of human history represents the time of the New Testament and the Christian era following it, in
which the death and sacrifice of Jesus has been seen as the redemption of
an original sin inherent in human nature. The third historic stage, in
which one "sacrifices God for nothingness," announces the advent of
Nihilism in Nietzsche's sense.

Here, we see how deeply and uniquely Nietzsche's Nihilism is rooted
in an historical awareness of human destiny. It is, however, note-
worthy that Nietzsche regards Christian morality, at least hitherto, as
"support" to preserve the integrity of human existence and as a "great
antidote" (Nietzsche, 1906: 11) for Nihilism. For Christian morality, in
Nietzsche's view, provides humanity an absolute value to counteract
the meaninglessness of human life, and served as an advocate for
God against suffering and evil in this world. Thus, for Nietzsche,
Christianity (as well as metaphysics) has had biological utility in the
sense that it was an invention useful to preserve human beings, an
inversion of the instinct for self-preservation inherent in human
beings. Yet, Nietzsche believed that in Christianity (and metaphysics)
there was a latent fiction, indispensable to human life, which "deceives
oneself in an effective way" (Nietzsche, 1906: 11). Now, however, according to Nietzsche, the time has ended when Christianity (and metaphysics) could have utility for human beings. This alludes to the arrival
of the third stage, in which one should "sacrifice God for nothingness." Is it not being honest to one's life, upon realizing that
faith in God is an unconscious fiction invented by the more basic will,
the "Will to Power," that one consciously returns to and takes one's
ground on the "Will to Power" as such? Thus, Nietzsche declares that
God is dead, and announces the advent of Nihilism, in the realization of
which one ought to endure, without palliatives, meaninglessness—without God.

I would suggest that we distinguish two forms of Nihilism, that is, "Nihilism before religion" and "Nihilism beyond religion."[3] The term Nihilism is often understood as a standpoint from which one recognizes the meaninglessness of human life, denying everything, including the existence of God. It is this naive Nihilism which declares that there is no God. I call this "Nihilism before religion" because it is a realization of the meaninglessness of life before definitive religious experience, and it therefore may be overcome by religion when one really comes to have a genuine religious experience. This form is found universally in human history and is a recurrent theme in both Eastern and Western thought.

Nietzsche's Nihilism, however, though equally godless, declares "God is dead" rather than "God is not." The statement "God is dead" can be rightly uttered only by those for whom God *was alive,* that is, by those who have lived religion. Nietzsche came to advocate Nihilism through the clear realization of the "depreciation" (*Unwertung*) of the traditional religious values of the past, including those of Christianity. For Nietzsche, Nihilism is a realization of the nothingness or meaninglessness of human life, not before, but through and after religion. Thus Nietzsche's Nihilism cannot be overcome by religion, at least in its traditional form. This is why I call Nietzsche's Nihilism "Nihilism beyond religion."

Nietzsche's Nihilism, declaring "God is dead," strikes at the core of traditional religion. He negates religion not simply from the outside, but from within. This is why in my paper "Buddhism and Christianity as a Problem of Today" I stated: "Nihilism, though it may not yet be a conspicuous historic power (as Scientism and Marxism), should be regarded as a sharp dagger pointed at the very heart of religion, because it radically negates religion, threatening to destroy it in its innermost cores" (Abe, 1963).

Although Nietzsche criticizes Christianity exclusively, all religions, including Buddhism, lie exposed to his attack. Now that Nietzsche's Nihilism is so influential, it seems to me almost meaningless for us, without confronting his Nihilism, to speak of a religion just as a religion, as something self-evident. It is now, therefore, an especially inescapable task for religions to be inquiring whether Nietzsche's Nihilism is really "Nihilism *beyond* religion" and to assume the burden of demonstrating, practically and theoretically, the *raison d'être* of religion.

It is only against the background of the problem of Scientism and Nihilism that the dialogue between Buddhism and Christianity can become truly significant and creative. Let me now propose how Buddhism and Christianity can confront these issues, and at the same time let me propose how the two religions can respectively open up a deeper religious dimension in which they can share a much greater spirituality than now.

Christianity

The following excerpt from the Epistle to the Philippians is for me one of the most impressive and touching passages in the Bible:

> Have this mind among yourselves, which you have in Christ Jesus, who, though he was in the form of God, did not count equality with God a thing to be grasped, but emptied himself, taking the form of a servant, being in the likeness of man. And being found in human form he humbled himself and became obedient unto death, even death on a cross (Phil 2:5–8).

There are two reasons for my appreciation of this passage. First, although Christ existed in the form of God, that is, being of the same divine nature as God, he refused to seize for his own the glory which belonged to God. Instead, he abdicated his divine rank and assumed the form of a servant, and, further, "he humbled himself and became obedient unto death, even death on a cross." This is the complete abnegation of Christ as the Son of God.

Second, this abnegation of Christ indicates the self-sacrificial love of Christ for humankind, disobedient to and in rebellion against the Will of God. Through the incarnation or *kenosis* the death and resurrection of Christ, God the Father reveals himself in terms of unconditional love beyond discriminatory justice. The infathomable depth of God's love is clearly realized when we come to know and believe that Christ as the Son of God emptied himself and became obedient to the point of death on the cross.

According to *The Interpreter's Bible* (*comm. in loc.*), at one time there was a theological debate "which turned largely on the question of how far Christ had ceased to be God when he became human. Did he strip himself entirely of the divine nature, or merely forgo certain attributes of majesty?" In my view, however, such a theological debate misses the point. Christ's *kenosis* and his abnegation must be understood not as partial, but as complete and thoroughgoing. As *The Interpreter's Bible* states: "He (Paul) says only that Christ *emptied himself*" and emphasizes "the full identity of Christ with the race of men."

Death of ego-self

Further, I think that this doctrine of Christ's *kenosis* should not be understood to mean that Christ was *originally* the Son of God and *then* emptied himself and became identical with man. Such a view in the temporal order, or the sequential order, is nothing but a conceptual and objectified understanding of the issue, not an experiential and religious understanding. Instead, we should understand the doctrine of Christ's *kenosis* to mean that Christ as the Son of God is *essentially* and *fundamentally* self-emptying or self-negating—because of this fundamental nature, the Son of God *is* Christ, that is, the Messiah. It is not that the Son of God *became* a man through the process of his self-emptying but that fundamentally he *is* true man and true God at one and the same time in this dynamic work and function of self-emptying.

Consequently, we may reformulate the doctrine of Christ's *kenosis* as follows:

> The Son of God is not the Son of God (for he is essentially and fundamentally self-emptying). Precisely because he *is not* the Son of God he *is* truly the Son of God (for he originally and always works as Christ, the Messiah, in his salvational function of self-emptying).

If we speak of *homoousion* indicating an identity of the full divinity and full humanity of Jesus Christ in one person, it must not simply signify the consubstantiality of two substances, divine and human, as it is traditionally understood, but rather a single or *nondual function* of self-emptying or self-negation. Without the profoundly dynamic nondual function of self-emptying the consubstantiality of the divinity and the humanity in Jesus Christ cannot be properly understood.

All that has been said about Christ the Son of God will be meaningless religiously if it is taken apart from the problem of human ego, or our own existential problem of the self. The notion of Christ's *kenosis* or his self-emptying can be properly understood only through the realization of our own sinfulness and our own existential self-denying. Jesus himself emphasizes: "He that finds his life shall lose it, and he that loses his life for my sake shall find it" (Mt 10:39). And Paul says: "Even so reckon you also yourselves to be dead unto sin, but alive unto God in Christ Jesus" (Rom 6:11). We are "always bearing about in the body the dying of Jesus, that the life also of Jesus may be manifested in our body" (2 Cor 4:10). These words of Jesus and Paul clearly show that the denial of our life, or the death of our ego-self because of our sinfulness, is necessary for our new life in Christ Jesus. This denial of our life or the death of our ego-self should not be partial but total and complete. Without the total negation of our life or the complete death of our ego-self, our new life as a manifestation of the life of Jesus is impossible. There can be no continuity between the "old person" and the "new person" in the Pauline faith. If one believes that the self as taught by Christianity continues somehow between the "old person" and the "new person," the religious significance of the self-emptying and abnegation of Christ, that is, the death and resurrection of Jesus, is not fully grasped.

Just as the self-emptying or abnegation of the Son of God must not be partial but total and thoroughgoing for him to be Christ, the self-denial or death of the human ego-self must not be partial but also total and complete. Only then can the new person be realized as the true and authentic self who confesses "it is no longer I that live, but Christ liveth in me: and that *life* which I now live in the flesh I live in the faith, the *faith* which is in the Son of God, who loved me, and gave himself up for me" (Gal 2:20).

Accordingly, can we not reformulate the notion of the new person as the true self who resurrects through the death of the old person in such a way that:

Self is not self (for self as the old person must die on account of its sin). Precisely because it is not self, self is truly self (for self is now alive as the new person, together with Christ).

This is especially the case, when we recall the following passages: "As in Adam all die, so also in Christ all shall be made alive" (1 Cor 15:22) and "Faithful is the saying: if we die with him, we shall also live with him" (2 Tim 2:11). Or, in our faith in Jesus as Christ, we die together with Christ day by day and are revived together with Christ day by day (1 Cor 15:31; 2 Cor 4:16). Every day, therefore, indeed, today, here and now, we die as the old person and resurrect as the new person with Christ. In this absolute present, we can properly say: "Self is not self, and precisely because it is not self, self is truly self."

Now, we have two formulations. First, in relation to the Son of God, we have said:

The Son of God is not the Son of God (for he is essentially and fundamentally self-emptying). Precisely because he *is not* the Son of God he *is* truly the Son of God (for he originally and

always works as Christ, the Messiah, in his salvational function
of self-emptying).

Second, in relation to the human self, we can say,

> Self is not self (for self as the old person must die on account of
> its sin). Precisely because it is not self, self is truly self (for self is
> now alive as the new person, together with Christ).

These two formulations stand together, signifying the two aspects of one
living reality—that is, faith in Jesus Christ.

With regard to the *kenosis* of Christ, however, there is an important
point for Christian faith which one should not overlook. The passage
from Philippians already quoted (2:5–8) continues as follows:

> Therefore God has highly exalted him and bestowed on him the
> name which is above every name, that at the name of Jesus
> every knee should bow, in heaven and on earth and under the
> earth, and every tongue confess that Jesus Christ is Lord, to the
> glory of God the Father (Phil 2:9–11).

This is the exaltation of Christ, whereas the *kenosis* in the previous
passage speaks of the humiliation of Christ. Precisely as a result of his
humiliation, Christ was raised to a yet higher place than he had before.
"The way he took was that of self-denial and entire obedience, and by so
acting he won his sovereignty" (*Interpreter's Bible, comm. in loc.*). In
order to understand the *kenosis* of Christ properly we must clearly recognize both his humiliation and his exaltation. I shall not, however, at this
point, discuss his exaltation.

What I now wish to ask is: if the Son of God empties himself, should
we not consider the self-emptying of God the Father, that is, the *kenosis*
of God himself? This is not merely a theological question, but an existential and religious question deeply rooted in Christian faith.

Christian theology generally states that the Son of God became
human without God ceasing to be God. In *Does God Exist?* Hans
Küng says:

> The distinction of the Son of God from God the Father, his
> obedience and subordination to the Father, is of course upheld
> everywhere in the New Testament. The Father is "greater" than

he is and there are things that are known only to the Father and
not to him. Neither is there any mention anywhere in the New
Testament of the incarnation of God himself (pages 684–685).

Küng also clearly says, "We should not of course speak of a 'crucified God'. That would suggest that God the Father, and not the Son, had
been crucified:—But we can and may certainly speak of a 'hidden God
revealed in the Crucified' " (Küng, 1980: 690–691).[4] As a Buddhist, however, who is concerned with promoting Buddhist-Christian dialogue in
order to explore a new and deeper religious dimension in the contemporary context of religion versus anti-religious ideologies, I realize that the
issue of the *kenosis* of God is a crucial issue. Is it not that the *kenosis,* the
self-emptying, of the Son of God has its origin in God the Father himself,
that is, the *kenosis* of God? Without the self-emptying of God the Father,
the self-emptying of the Son of God is inconceivable. In the case of
Christ, *kenosis* is realized in the fact that one who was in the form of God
emptied himself and assumed the form of a servant. It originated in the
will of God and the love of God which is willing to forgive even the sinner
who has rebelled against him. It was a deed that was accomplished on the
basis of God's *will.* On the other hand, in the case of God, *kenosis* is
implied in the original *nature* of God, that is love (Nishitani, 1982: 59;
Moltmann, 1972). And my emphasis on the *kenosis* of God himself
seems to be supported by Karl Rahner, when he says in *Foundations of
Christian Faith:*

> The primary phenomenon given by faith is precisely the self-
> emptying of God, his becoming, the kenosis and genesis of God
> himself.—In so far as in his abiding and infinite fullness he
> empties himself, the other comes to be as God's very own real-
> ity. The phrase is already found in Augustine that God "as-
> sumes by creating" and also "creates by assuming," that is, he
> creates by emptying himself, and therefore, of course, he him-
> self is in the emptying (Rahner, 1978: 222).

In his article in *Sacramentum Mundi,* under the title, "Jesus' death as the
death of God," Karl Rahner emphasizes the death of Jesus as the death of
God by saying that:

> Christology at the present day must reflect more closely on
> Jesus' death, not only in its redemptive effect, but also in itself.

—If it is said that the incarnate Logos died only in his human reality, and if this is tacitly understood to mean that this death therefore did not affect God, only half the truth has been stated. The really Christian truth has been omitted.—Our 'possessing' God must repeatedly pass through the deathly abandonment by God (Matt 27:46; Mark 15:34) in which alone God ultimately comes to us, because God has given himself in love and as love, and thus is realized, and manifested in his death, Jesus' death belongs to God's self-utterance (Rahner, 1969: 3; 207f).

Reading Karl Rahner more closely, however, I find an important point which I cannot accept. Referring to the mystery of the incarnation, Rahner says:

God can become something. He who is not subject to change in himself can *himself* be subject to change *in something else.*— The absolute One God in the pure freedom of his infinite unre- latedness, which he always preserves, possesses the possibility of himself becoming the other, the finite. He possesses the possibil- ity of *establishing* the other as his own reality by dispossessing *himself,* by giving *himself* away.—God goes out of himself, he himself, he as the self-giving fullness. Because he can do this, because this is his free and primary possibility, for this reason he is defined in scripture as love (Rahner, 1978: 220).

Although these statements emphasize the self-emptying of God himself, they still leave behind traces of dualism, a dualism of God and the other, the infinite and the finite, immutability and change, within and without, and so forth. Of course, this is not a simple dualism in the ordinary sense, because God is understood here to possess "the possibility of himself becoming the other, the finite"—"by dispossessing himself."

This dynamic interpretation of God, however, implies two things. First, by virtue of love God does not remain in his infinite unrelatedness but goes out of himself and gives himself away to the other. Second, even so, as the absolute One, God "always preserves" his infinite unrelated- ness. This implies that God's infinite unrelatedness has priority over his relatedness with the other. Again, God's infinite fullness, being abiding, has priority over his self-emptying. This is clearly seen in Rahner's state- ment "insofar as in his abiding and infinite fullness he empties himself, the other comes to be as God's very own reality" (Rahner, 1978: 221).

This is where I see traces of dualism. Are these traces of dualism absolutely necessary for Christian faith in God? Do these traces of dualism have a positive rather than negative significance in Christianity? Rahner himself emphasizes that "the primary phenomenon given by faith is precisely the self-emptying of God, his becoming, the kenosis and genesis of God himself" (Rahner, 1978: 222). If this is the case, then traces of dualism must not only be minimized, they must be eliminated. God's self-emptying must be understood not to be partial but total, to the extent that his infinite unrelatedness has no priority over his relatedness with the other and that his self-emptying is dynamically identical with his abiding and infinite fullness.

Since we do not see this kind of *total* self-emptying of God in Rahner's interpretation, I cannot help but say that even for Karl Rahner, the *kenosis* of God, God's self-emptying, is still somewhat conceptualized or objectified. If God is really unconditional love, his self-emptying must be total, not partial. It must not be that God *becomes something else* by his partial self-giving, but that in and through his total self-emptying God *is* something—or more precisely, God *is* each and every thing. This emphasis, however, should not be taken to signify pantheism. On the contrary, only through this total *kenosis* and his self-sacrificial identification with everything in the world is God truly God. Here, the reality and actuality of God, which is entirely beyond conception and objectification, is fully realized. This *kenotic* God is the ground of the *kenotic* Christ. God is not truly God if God the Father continues to be God in the self-emptying of the Son of God.

Accordingly, concerning faith in God, it must be said:

> God is not God (for he is love and completely self-emptying); precisely because he is not (self-affirmative) God, God is truly God of love (for through complete self-abnegation God is totally identical with everything including sinful man).

This means that *kenosis* or emptying is not an attribute (however important it may be) of God, but the fundamental *nature* of God himself. God is God, not because he had the Son of God take a human form and be sacrificed, while he himself remained God, but because he himself is a suffering God, a self-sacrificial God through his total *kenosis*. The *kenotic* God who totally empties himself and totally sacrifices himself is, in my view, true God. And it is precisely this *kenotic* God who thoroughly saves everything including human beings and nature, through his self-sacrificial, abnegating love. I also believe that the notion of *kenotic* God can overcome Nietzsche's Nihilism which insists upon the need to "sacrifice God for nothing," because instead of being sacrificed by radical nihilists in the third stage of human history for nothingness, the *kenotic* God sacrifices himself not for relative nothingness but for *absolute* nothingness which is at one and the same time absolute Being.

God's total *kenosis* is not God's self-sacrifice for something else or God's self-negation for nihilistic nothingness, but God's self-sacrifice for absolutely "nothing" other than his own fulfillment. Only in God's total *kenosis,* everything including the unjust and sinner, natural and moral evil, is forgiven, and redeemed and satisfied, and thus the love of God is completely fulfilled. The notion of a *kenotic* God thus goes beyond Nietzsche's radical Nihilism by deepening the religious significance of the Christian notion of the love of God. In addition, the notion of *kenotic* God opens up for Christianity a common ground with Buddhism by overcoming Christianity's monotheistic character, the absolute oneness of God, and by sharing with Buddhism the realization of Absolute Nothingness as the essential realization of the ultimate. This can be accomplished through the notion of a *kenotic* God—not through losing Christianity's self-identity, but rather through deepening its spirituality.

Furthermore, the notion of a *kenotic* God can also find room for the autonomous reason of modern science and the rationalistic subjectivity of the modern world because, in the notion of a *kenotic* God who is totally self-emptying, God's infinite unrelatedness and abiding fullness (which are incompatible with autonomous reason and modern man's rationalistic subjectivity) are eliminated. And yet, through his total self-emptying, God is believed to reveal his love most profoundly to embrace even a person's ego-self which stands against God with its autonomous reason. However, insofar as a person's ego-self remains with itself, a *kenotic* God is not really understood by it. Only when ego-self negates itself completely does it come to understand who a *kenotic* God is and what God's total self-emptying means to the self. Accordingly, the above statement, "God is not God, precisely because he is not (self-affirmative) God, God is truly God," can be properly grasped by the parallel existential realization that, "Self is not self, precisely because it is not self is truly self."

Buddhism

Now, we will turn to Buddhism and discuss how Buddhism can overcome scientism and Nietzsche's Nihilism on the one hand, and, on the other hand, how Buddhism can open up a common dimension for dialogue with Christianity.

The ultimate reality for Buddhism is Shunyata. The word literally means "emptiness" or "voidness" and can imply "absolute nothingness." This is because Shunyata is entirely unobjectifiable and unconceptualizable. As such it cannot be any sort of a 'thing'. Accordingly, if Shunyata is conceived *somewhere outside* one's self-existence it is not true Shunyata any longer because Shunyata conceived outside one's existence turns into *something* represented and called by oneself "Shunyata." Throughout its long history, Mahayana Buddhism has strongly rejected views of Shunyata such as a "literal understanding of negativity," a "view of annihilatory nothingness" or "the emptiness perversely clung to." Instead, it emphasizes that "Shunyata is Non-Shunyata (*ashūnyatā*); therefore it is ultimate Shunyata (*atyānta-shūnyatā*)."[5] Accordingly, however important the notion of Shunyata may be in Buddhism, after Martin Heidegger, who wrote *Sein* 'under erasure' so as to show the unobjectifiability of S~~ei~~n, we also write Shunyata under erasure (i.e. Shu~~ny~~ata). This indicates that true Shunyata is not Shunyata as we can think about it, but Shunyata lived by us so that self and Shunyata are dynamically identical. Consequently, although the term Shunyata sounds negative it has positive religious (or soteriological) meanings.

The positive and soteriological meanings of Shunyata are, summarily, four.

First, in Shunyata, regardless of the distinction between self and other, person and nature, human and divine, everything without exception is realized *as it is* in its *Suchness*. Like Christianity, Buddhism is primarily concerned with salvation, but, unlike Christianity, Buddhism does not take the personalistic divine-human relationship as the *basis* of salvation, regarding nature as something peripheral, but takes as the *basis* of salvation, the transpersonal, universal dimension common to person and nature (Abe, 1985: 212). Furthermore, unlike Christianity which talks about God as the savior, Buddhism does not accept the notion of a savior outside of one's self. Buddha is none other than one who awakens to Dharma, that is, everything's Suchness, in the realization of Shunyata. This means that Suchness realized in Shunyata encompasses everything including human beings, nature, and the divine, and that the realization of Suchness entails awakening to one's original nature and emancipation from attachment.

Secondly, Shunyata is *boundless openness* without any center. Shunyata is free from anthropocentrism, cosmocentrism and theocentrism (Abe, 1985: 211). Only in this way is Emptiness possible. Accordingly, in Shunyata there is no dominant-subordinate relationship (i.e., subject-object relationship) between things. The person is not subordinate to the Buddha, nor is nature subordinate to the person. Everything, without exception, is dominant over everything else and at the same time subordinate to everything else. This is complete emancipation and freedom from any kind of bondage resulting from discrimination. If, in Christianity, as I suggested earlier, the *kenosis* of God the Father is fully realized, and God himself completely empties himself, this dynamic relationship of mutual dominant-subordinate relationship or the mutual immanence and transcendence of humanity and God, and humanity and nature, can be fully realized. This would overcome the theocentrism innate in Christianity.

Thirdly, Shunyata implies *jinen* (Abe, 1985: 104, 150, 272, 273), a Sino-Japanese word meaning "so of itself" or "spontaneity." It also means "naturalness," not as a counter concept of human agency, but as the fundamental ground for both humanity and nature, for change in both human life and nature. Accordingly, *jinen* is beyond any kind of will, including human will, God's will, and will to power in Nietzsche's sense. But, *jinen* is not a motionless, static or dead state, but rather the most dynamic spontaneity because it is spontaneity realized in Shunyata without any will, self or other, human or divine. God's complete self-emptying as the absolute self-negation of the will of God must be based on this spontaneity in terms of *jinen*.

Fourthly, in Shunyata, there is both the interpenetration and the mutual reversibility of all things. This is a natural consequence of the previously mentioned mutuality of dominance and subordination of all things. The unity of opposites is fully realized in Shunyata because Shunyata is boundless openness without any center or circumference. Accordingly, not only spatial realities but also temporal realities, and even value judgments, are perceived as interpenetrating and reciprocal. In this dynamic of Shunyata great compassion and great wisdom interpenetrate and make possible the realization of nirvana in the midst of samsara.

To these four points, at least the following two criticisms may be raised by Christians. First, if past and future are completely interpenetrating and reciprocal, how can there be history? Secondly, if judgment, including the distinction between good and evil, is completely reciprocal or reversible, how can human ethics be established?

In addition to these criticisms, Christians may make the following point:

Christianity also talks about the interpenetration of past and
future, for example, in terms of creation and eschatology (i.e.,
continuous creation and realised eschatology) and talks about
the reversibility of value judgment, for example, in Jesus' words
"I came not to call the righteous, but sinners." In Christianity,
however, Jesus as the ruler of history provides a criterion for
ethical judgment and a goal for history.

My response to these criticisms is twofold. First, Shunyata should
not be understood as the goal or end of Buddhist life, but as the point of
departure from which Buddhist life and activity can properly begin.
Shunyata as the goal of Buddhist life is Shunyata conceived outside of
one's self-existence, which, as I have said, is not true Shunyata.

Secondly, Shunyata is fundamentally Non-Shunyata, that is, it is
Shunyata under erasure (Shuⱦyata). That is the true and ultimate Shunyata. This means that true Shunyata empties itself as well as everything
else. Through its self-emptying it makes everything exist as it is and work
as it does. Shunyata can better be understood as a verb rather than as a
noun, because it is a pure and dynamic *function* of all-emptying.

Conclusions

On the basis of these two basic considerations I would like to make
two critical reflections. First, in Buddhism the problem of free will has
never been grasped positively. This is a significant difference from the
Western tradition, wherein the importance of human free will has been
strongly emphasized. Only through free decision of free will can one's
subjectivity and personality be legitimately established. Buddhism has
regarded free will negatively. That is to say, in Buddhism the problem of
human free will is grappled with in terms of karma which must be overcome in order to achieve emancipation. And, emancipation from karma
does not lead us to the Will of God (as in Christianity), nor to the will to
power (as in Nietzsche), but rather to Shunyata, which is entirely beyond
any kind of will. It is *jinen,* that is, naturalness, or spontaneity without
will. Accordingly, how the principle of free will can be positively established in the locus of Shunyata is a serious and urgent issue for Buddhism today.

How can Shunyata, which is free from any centrism, focus itself
upon a particular center? How can Shunyata, as agentless spontaneity,

establish a personal God in its boundless openness? Unless this question is sufficiently resolved Buddhism cannot properly ground modern rationality nor overcome Nietzsche's principle of the will to power.

It is my view that in its self-emptying, Shunyata concentrates itself in a particular center which we may call "Vow" (Sanskrit: *praṇidhāna*). This is because the self-emptying of Shunyata is the compassionate aspect of Shunyata, while Shunyata as such is its wisdom aspect. It is Vow that is a particular center focused upon in Shunyata. Shunyata which does not transform itself into Vow is not true Shunyata. However, Shunyata which simply remains Vow is also not true Shunyata. True Shunyata must empty (or "shunyatize") even Vow and turn it into "act" or "deed" (Sanskrit: *charita* or *charyā*). A vow which is not acted upon cannot be called a true vow. In this way, in and through self-emptying, Shunyata always transforms itself into Vow and into Act, and then dynamically centralizes itself into a focal point.

Second, although Buddhism does not lack a characteristic view of time, it is very weak in its view of history (Abe, 1985: 314–315). This is simply because in Buddhism time is understood to be entirely beginningless and endless, and not irreversible but reversible. Accordingly, the undirectionality essential to the notion of history is not clearly grasped in Buddhism. This is a weakness of Buddhism as it confronts Christianity and the contemporary worldviews such as Marxism and Nietzschian Nihilism. Buddhism, however, can develop its own view of history, if we take seriously the compassionate aspect of Shunyata, that is, the self-emptying of Shunyata. In the wisdom aspect of Shunyata, everything is realized in its Suchness, in its interpenetration of and reciprocity with everything else. Time is no exception to this. Accordingly, in the light of wisdom realized in Shunyata past and future are interpenetrating and reciprocal, and the beginningless and endless process of time is totally concentrated in each moment. Because of this, in Buddhism, each moment, each "now," is realized as Eternal Now and Absolute Present.

In the light of compassion, also realized in Shunyata, another aspect of time comes to be realized. Although an Awakened One realizes everything and everyone in their Suchness and interpenetration in the light of wisdom, innumerable beings in the past and the future think themselves to be unenlightened and deluded. The task for an Awakened One is to help these people to awaken to their Suchness and interpenetration with all other things. This is the compassionate aspect of Shunyata which can be actualized only by "shunyatizing" the wisdom aspect of Shunyata.

This process of actualizing the compassionate aspect of Shunyata is end-less because people who believe themselves to be unenlightened will ap-pear endlessly.

Here the progress of history toward the future is necessary and comes to have a positive significance. In the light of wisdom realized in Shun-yata, everything and everyone are realized in their Suchness and time is overcome. In the light of compassion also realized in Shunyata, however, time is religiously significant and essential. And this endless process of compassionate work for an Awakened One to awaken others is no less than the above mentioned process of Shunyata turning itself into Vow and into Act through its self-emptying. Here, we have a Buddhist view of history. It is not, however, an eschatological or teleological view of history in the Christian or Western sense. In terms of eschatology, the Buddhist view of history is completely realized eschatology, because in the light of wisdom everything and everyone without exception are realized in their Suchness, and time is thereby overcome. In terms of teleology, the Bud-dhist view of history is an open teleology because in the light of compas-sion the process of awakening others in history is endless. And the completely realized eschatology and the entirely open teleology are dy-namically united in the Now.

True Shunyata is not static but dynamic—it is a pure and unceasing function of self-emptying, making self and others manifest their Such-ness. It is urgently necessary to grasp the notion of Shunyata dynamically in order to give new life to Buddhism in the contemporary world.

Summary

I have suggested that, in Christianity, the notion of the *kenotic* God is essential as the root-source of the *kenotic* Christ, if God is truly God of love. I have also suggested that in Buddhism, Shunyata must be grasped dynamically, not statically, since Shunyata indicates not only wisdom but also compassion. Then, when we clearly realize the notion of the *kenotic* God in Christianity and the notion of the dynamic Shunyata in Buddhism—without eliminating the distinctiveness of either religion but rather by deepening their respective uniqueness—we find a significant common basis at a more profound level. In this way, I believe, Christian-ity and Buddhism can enter into a profound and creative dialogue, by overcoming the anti-religious ideologies prevailing in our contemporary society.

Notes

1. A good example of this development is John Cobb's recent book, *Beyond Dialogue, Toward a Mutual Transformation of Christianity and Buddhism,* Fortress Press, Philadelphia, 1982.
2. This section on Nihilism is largely taken from Abe, 1968.
3. These may roughly correspond to Nietzsche's notion of "passive nihilism" and "active nihilism."
4. In his "Notes," Hans Küng calls the reader's attention to Moltmann's use of quotation marks, e.g. "The 'crucified God' " (the title of the important Chapter VI of Moltmann, 1972). See Küng, 1980: 793.
5. *Pañcavimśatisāhasrāprajñāpāramitā-sūtra* (Taishō Tripiṭaka, vol. 8, page 250 column b).

God's Self-Renunciation and Buddhist Emptiness: A Christian Response to Masao Abe

Hans Küng

Since the beginning of the profound crisis of contemporary European society around World War I, the "post-modern" world-order which has developed is no longer eurocentric, but post-colonial, post-imperialistic. Speaking more positively: we find ourselves moving into a multi-centered, trans-cultural, multi-religious paradigm. Outwardly, the European powers have lost the domination of the world which they achieved earlier, and, more profoundly, the socio-cultural driving forces of modernity which were released in the seventeenth century—science, technology, industry, and democracy—have met with difficulty and have lost their godlike status, together with the most honored of the gods, Progress. They are ensnared in a crisis.

Religion, which, because of its senseless opposition to modern science, technology, industry, and democracy, is increasingly oppressed and often severely persecuted, seems to have a new chance in post-modernity. Religious movements, together with other, alternative movements—civil rights, women's, peace, and environmentalist—once again burst forth throughout the world. It seems to me that this chance will be well-utilized only if this movement proves itself to be not simply a restoration (of the pre-modern, medieval) but an innovation (of the post-modern)—if religion is renewed not, as so often in the past, as a reactionary, repressive and regressive power of an intellectual minority, but is experienced as a future-oriented, instaurative power of individual and social liberation. As soon as liberation stands at the very center of both the

Buddhist and Christian messages, a new opportunity is certainly offered Buddhism and Christianity.

The situation of this paradigm change makes it clear how important the challenge of Masao Abe, along with John Cobb (the primary initiators of a Christian-Buddhist dialogue upon a new, scholarly base) is: the inter-religious dialogue is to be led in the socio-cultural context of the exchange between traditional religion and modern irreligiousness and, given that, a fundamental, new understanding of the religious message of Buddhism and Christianity must stand at the center of our efforts, so also must the other side of the horizon of contemporary history not escape our notice—including, indeed, the still virulent, modern religious criticism of a Feuerbach or Marx, a Nietzsche or Freud. Masao Abe in an impressive and original manner has made clear the entanglement of the problematic from the Buddhist standpoint, and I, as a Christian theologian, am pleased by the frequent concurrence: regarding the affirmation of rational science (which is fully consonant with religion) and the rejection of any anti-religious ideology of science—of modern scientism—but also regarding the epochal import of the contemporary criticism of Nietzsche and the necessity of overcoming the meaninglessness of life and history, of nihilism. To be sure, here is where our discussion opens, and, being challenged to respond from the Christian standpoint, I gladly face this astute and learned Buddhist discussion partner.

Nihilism as the Result of Modern Atheism

We agree: Nietzsche, without a doubt, skilfully analyzed European modernity. As Abe emphasizes in connection with Martin Heidegger: nihilism is the inner consequence of western history—but by all means not, I should qualify, the consequence of European antiquity, of the Middle Ages, or of the time of the Reformation; it is, instead, the consequence of the modernity which began in the seventeenth and eighteenth centuries, and which in the nineteenth and twentieth centuries subsequently fell into an utter crisis with the notorious "Dialectic of the Age of Enlightenment" (Adorno/Horkheimer). The crisis of modernity was noted by Nietzsche long before the First World War, together with a few other clear-sighted persons (above all, Kierkegaard and Dostoevsky) and he recognized his time, when European enthusiasm over progress was still at its zenith, as a time of decadence, of inner deterioration. Why? "The most important recent occurrence—that 'God is dead,' that the belief in the Christian God has become incredible—already begins to cast its first shadows over Europe": so begins Friedrich Nietzsche in the fifth book, "We, the Fearless," of his *A Gay Science* (Nietzsche, 1954–6: 2; 205). Casting a shadow over Europe: but not only Europe! Like a warning to the countries of Asia, who find themselves, more than anyone else today, in the frenzy of modernization—it speaks to us today when Nietzsche adds: "The decline of belief in the Christian God is an incident which concerns all of Europe, in which all peoples shall have their share of benefit and honor" (Nietzsche, 1954–6: 2; 227).

So what are the consequences of modern atheism? The result in the near future is—we recall the oppressive and repressive form of religion during the Ancien Régime—an inexpressible brightening, unburdening, invigoration, encouragement, a new dawn, a broader horizon, the open sea; however, the consequences of this enormous occurrence in the more distant future are, according to Nietzsche, gloomier, though the rationalistic optimists of progress don't want this to be true. The "insane man" describes, according to him, something which only scarcely allows itself to be rendered in terms: "How were we able to drink the sea? Who gave us the sponge to erase the horizon? What did we do when we unchained this earth from its sun? Whither does it now move?" (Nietzsche, 1954–6: 2; 127). God's death signifies, then, the great collapse! Wretched vacuity: a drained sea. A hopeless environment: the erased horizon. Abysmal nothingness: the earth unchained from the sun. For the individual, a deadly plunge without orientation in any direction, which necessarily ruptures him: "Where are we going? Away from all suns? Are we not dashing perpetually onward? Backwards, sideways, forwards, in all directions?" (Nietzsche, 1954–6: 2; 127). Here is chaos unfolding, yes, the deadly cold and night of Nihilism: "Is there still an above and below? Are we not lost as in an unending nothingness? Does the void not breathe its breath upon us? Has it not become colder? Does night and more night approach unceasingly?" (Nietzsche, 1954–6: 2; 127).

Thereby it is made clear: modern nihilism is not, as Abe says, the consequence of religion, at least not directly. It is the consequence of religious deficiency, of irreligiousness, of atheism. And modern humanity has indeed "offered God as a sacrifice to Nothingness," but has also paid a great price therefor with the hell of world wars, of concentration camps, and of Solzhenitsyn's Gulag, with the desolation or meaninglessness of life. The Buddhist cannot be pleased with this, for a Buddhist—inasmuch as he participates in modernity—is also affected. And Masao Abe is correct when he sees an absence of Christianity and Buddhism in Nihilism. Not only in modern Europe, but also in modern Japan, religion has been replaced by a pseudo-religion (nationalism and militarism)—with catastrophic consequences for Japan's neighbors and ultimately for Japan itself. Nietzsche was of the opinion that not only belief in God itself, but also all the consequences of belief in God must be overcome. God is dead, but His shadow is long: "After the Buddha was dead, people displayed his shadow for centuries afterwards in a cave—a ghastly shadow. God is dead: but such is the nature of humanity that perhaps for millennia there will be caves in which his shadow will be displayed. And we—we, too, still have to conquer his shadow" (Nietzsche, 1954–6: 2; 115).

Yet, Friedrich Nietzsche—patient, critic, and therapist of the fatal illness: nihilism—was not truly able to conquer nihilism—neither with his message of the superperson and of the reevaluation of all values nor with the idea of the conquest of the eternal return of the shadow God's likeness. Certainly, to the extent that Nietzsche exposed nihilism as a consequence of modern atheism, he proved himself a precise analyst of the end of modernity. However, insofar as he proclaimed the death of God without the possibility of resurrection, he proved himself a false predicter, who, demented from 1889, was not even able to witness post-modernity.

Nietzsche's criticism of religion sought also to strike at Buddhism, which he understood as "passive Nihilism" (*Der Fall Wagner;* Nietzsche, 1954–6: 2; 901–938). It must be supplanted with active nihilism, a nihilism of strength.

The "most extreme form of nihilism" is, according to him, "the insight," "that *every* belief, everything held to be true is necessarily false: because there is no *real world*" (*Ecce homo:* Nietzsche, 1954–6: 2; 1141).

But is there actually no "real world"; is there no "God"? Certainly there is no longer "God" according to Nietzsche in the "traditional form" of another world (here Masao Abe is correct): no longer in the sense of a Platonic, and also often Christian dualism, where God and world are separated. But is this the only alternative? Is it impossible and spurious to conceive of God's being *in* the world and the world *in* God? Even Nietzsche's philosophy uses unproved hypotheses and constructions, and his structure of history from the end of modernity to atheism and nihilism—at the current threshold of post-modernity—allows itself to be turned around. How? I would like to illustrate this in a manner similar to Abe's in connection with an earlier work (*Does God Exist?* [ET: New

York, 1980], pp. 613–615), by using a text from Nietzsche which opposes
the Platonic "real world," and which is yet more aggressive than that
advanced by Abe.

From Modern Nihilism to Post-Modern Belief in God

In Nietzsche's *Twilight of the Idols,* which appeared after his collapse, he briefly describes the history of the disintegration of the "real
world," as it was established by Plato and passed on to the future by
Christianity, was afterward deflated by Kant and left behind by Positivism as an unknown quantity, and was finally fully abolished by Nihilism,
and creatively overcome through the Dionysian "Yes" to all uncertain-
ties—this all under the title of "How the 'Real World' Finally Became a
Fable: The History of an Error":

1. The real world, attainable to the wise, the pious, the virtuous
   man—he dwells in it, *he is it.*
   (Oldest form of the idea, relatively sensible, simple, con-
   vincing.
   Transcription of the proposition 'I, Plato *am* the truth'.)
2. The real world, unattainable for the moment, but promised
   to the wise, the pious, the virtuous man ('to the sinner who
   repents'.)
   (Progress of the idea: it grows more refined, more enticing,
   more incomprehensible—*it becomes a woman,* it becomes
   Christian.)
3. The real world, unattainable, undemonstrable, cannot be
   promised, but even when merely thought of a consolation, a
   duty, an imperative.
   (Fundamentally the same old sun, but shining through
   mist and scepticism; the idea grown sublime, pale, moth-
   erly, Konigsbergian.)
4. The real world—unattainable? Unattained, at any rate. And
   if unattained also *unknown.* Consequently also no consolation, no redemption, no duty: how could we have a duty
   towards something unknown?
   (The grey of dawn. First yawnings of reason. Cockcrow of
   positivism.)
5. The 'real world'—an idea no longer of any use, not even a

duty any longer—an idea grown useless, superfluous, *consequently* a refuted idea: let us abolish it!

(Broad daylight; breakfast; return of cheerfulness and *bon sens;* Plato blushes for shame; all free spirits run riot.)

6. We have abolished the real world: what world is left? The apparent world perhaps?. . . But no! *with the real world we have also abolished the apparent world!*

(Mid-day; moment of the shortest shadow; end of the longest error; zenith of mankind; INCIPIT ZARATHUS-TRA.)

Is this an end . . . or a turning point? A succession of scenes sparkling and scintillating with wit, irony and malice, provoking us to reverse the series? Might it not be possible to turn Nietzsche's "history of an error" back to front—so to speak—into a new future? The new title might be *"The* (future) *history of a* (newly discovered) *truth"*:

6. The idea of God—it cannot be abolished. Humanity never reached that peak. Zarathustra turned out to be a myth.

(Twilight of the superperson—end of the briefest error; no replacement of religion by science.)

5. The idea of God, of no further use, no longer binding, even superfluous, shows signs of new life.

(Nihilism—particularly for the *bon sens* of the truly liberated spirits—an unproved idea. Joy among the angels. Red faces among the devils.)

4. The idea of God, certainly unattainable by pure reason and unknown in its reality, nevertheless begins again to be consoling, redeeming, binding.

(The gray of dawn. The last yawnings of reason as it becomes aware of itself; positivism awakes from its illusions.)

3. The idea of God not only as imperative a la Konigsberg or as feeble consolation for the weak.

(Fundamentally the same old sun, but shining afresh through mist and skepticism as reality and great promise: no remythicization.)

2. The idea of God now attainable, not only for the virtuous, the pious, the wise, but also for the culpable, the irreligious, the "sinners".

> (Progress of the idea; bright day; enlightenment of the
> world by faith; return of the Christian reality. The idea of
> God becomes more comprehensible, more straightfor-
> ward, more concrete, more human.)
> 1. The idea of God perceptible, relatively simple and convinc-
>   ing: the God of Israel. Oldest form of the idea. He, Jesus,
>   dwells in it, *he is it.* Transcription of the proposition: "I *am*
>   the way, the truth and the life."
>   (Noon; moment of the briefest shade; beginning of eternal
>   truth; peak of humanity. INCIPIT REGNUM DEI.)

Hence: not only the God of philosophers and scholars in the pallor of
thought (Descartes), but the living God as the "Not-other" (Nicholas of
Cusa) and yet "wholly Other" (Barth, Horkheimer), as the truly "more
divine God" (Heidegger). Not only a *causa sui* (Spinoza) but "the God of
Abraham, Isaac and Jacob, the God of Jesus Christ" (Pascal).

Thus in the end truth could become fable and fable truth. A turning
away from the atheistic antithesis to a new "theistic," Judeo-Christian
synthesis. A vision? A projection? An illusion? A suggestion? A hope—
not more, but also not less?

As always: these reflections upon Nietzsche and nihilism now allow
me passage to a deeper level, to reflections about the kenosis of God, the
humiliation, renunciation, the emptying of God, which is linked by
Masao Abe in an illuminating manner with the Emptiness of Buddhism.
But the question poses itself to the Christian theologian as follows.

The Kenosis of God Himself?

Masao Abe gives, it is quite clear, his own Buddhist interpretation of
the hymn found in the Epistle to the Philippians (Phil 2: 5–8, possibly
pre-Paul and later recast by Paul)—a Bible passage especially impressive
and moving for Abe. If I might immediately get to the decisive point of
his detailed interpretation: the kenosis, humiliation, renunciation, emptying of Jesus Christ by the crucifixion is to be understood, according to
Abe, as the kenosis, renunciation, emptying *of God Himself,* completely
and radically, which accords in a non-dualist sense with the renunciation
of ourselves in the unity of non-duality.

That is: emptying is the basic nature of God Himself. Not only the
Son of God, no, God empties Himself completely of His divinity. And
this is to be understood not objectively like a temporal-historical occur-

rence, but religiously and empirically as an essential-eternal state of affairs. So can the kenotic God of the Christians ultimately be replaced by the all-inclusive (dynamic) Emptiness (shunyata) of the Buddhists. Indeed, the absoluteness of God can be equated with its relativity, the Nature of God with every individual thing and, similarly, the unending abundance with its unending emptiness! From this respect, the outcome of Masao Abe's paradox is in accord: God is not God; and exactly because He is not God, he is truly God. A God and Father who has not fully renounced Himself in his self-sacrifice is not the true God.

But of course the question suggests itself: Can this ingenious Buddhist interpretation also be the Christian interpretation? Does it faithfully render the text? In my book, *The Incarnation of God* (T. and T. Clark, Edinburgh 1987), which has finally appeared in English, I grappled with this difficulty in the context of Hegelian philosophy. I must, however, limit myself here. Masao Abe himself draws attention to decisive points, which can only be acknowledged and clarified here:

1. In the New Testament, the term "God" (*ho theos* = God, purely and simply) for all practical purposes always means the one God and Father and never a divine nature consisting of several persons.

2. The man, Jesus of Nazareth, is the likeness or Son of God's Word rather than a likeness of Christ or of God's Messiah.

3. In the entire New Testament (and in principle also in the later Doctrine of the Trinity) the distinction of God's Son from God the Father, and the subordination of the Son under Him who is "greater" than He, is steadfastly maintained.

4. Consequently, nowhere is there mentioned an incarnation or a renunciation (kenosis) of God Himself; the Philippian hymn only speaks of a kenosis of Jesus Christ, the Son of God. Furthermore, this kenosis is not understood as a permanent status, position, relationship, but as a humiliation occurring in a unique, historical life and death on the cross. Even the Hellenistic congregation of Philippi (more interested in the divinity of Jesus than was the original Jewish congregation) was less interested in a divine Christ than in the event of the humiliation and renunciation initiated by God.

5. Certainly, the self-sacrifice of the Son does not occur against the will of the Father. God desires the redemption of humanity and so also the self-sacrifice of Jesus. Still, God the Father does not give Himself up, but His Son (the church condemns the monophysitic "patripassianism"), and so God the Father (*ho theos*) does not die upon the cross, but the man, Jesus of Nazareth, the Son of God. Only He, not God Himself, is

(according to the dying words of Jesus quoting Psalm 22:1 [Vulgate 21:1]) forsaken by God! Jesus being forsaken by God is, according to the New Testament, no divine "paradox," but human agony crying to heaven.

6. Given this, it seems to me—and Abe appropriately quotes my criticism of Jurgen Moltmann's Christology—that the discussion about the "crucified God" and that of a "killed" or "dead" God is unbiblical. The Buddhist appropriately places the question before those Christian theologians (also Karl Rahner), who in an unbiblical (in fact monophysitic or Hegelian) manner speak of the kenosis of God Himself: must not they themselves, given God's truly successful emptying of Himself (His death), consequently have to confess the Emptiness of Buddhism?

7. The stumbling-block of a (Buddhist or Christian) Christology (and Trinitarian Doctrine) which completely identifies Jesus with God and brazenly declares Jesus' death to be the death of God is made strikingly clear in the case of the resurrection: such a Christology cannot explain who brought this supposedly dead God back to life.

8. According to the hymn in Philippians, it is (as in the entire New Testament) quite unequivocally God Himself, the Father, who awakened the man, Jesus of Nazareth, His Son and Messiah, to eternal life, and exalted Him. This is the significant flaw in Masao Abe's interpretation: he indeed makes reference to the resurrection, but practically speaking neglects it—has to neglect it. Why? In order to be able to abide by his interpretation: the renunciation of God Himself in Buddhist shunyata. A very basic question arises here: the question of the effective hermeneutic for this inter-religious dialogue.

The True Dialogical Hermeneutic?

There is no question: Masao Abe's basic intention is dialogic. He isolates key concepts from Christian texts which he then transplants into a Buddhist context, where the concept of kenosis is understood not simply as ethical, exemplary humiliation, but is recast as ontological emptying, an emptying of God, Himself, yes, ultimately as Emptiness in general, shunyata. In this manner, as a Buddhist, he discovers his own world—even on foreign, Christian soil. Just as the Christian authors earlier gave a Christian exegesis of Greek or Buddhist texts, so also Abe gives a Buddhist exegesis of the Christian texts. He wants in this manner to overcome the cultural and religious gap. Both of these religious traditions seem closer than hitherto had been assumed.

But: is this an adequate hermeneutic for the inter-religious dialogue?

Basically nothing personal is at stake because, even in foreign raiment, one finds only one's own world again. Is such a dialogical hermeneutic not truly selective and reductive? It becomes clear with the example of the Epistle to the Philippians: one chooses from the context of the Christian scriptures only a few welcome passages and ignores the rest (it is selective), then interprets these passages according to one's personal interest (it is reductive). Indeed, such a hermeneutic—whether Buddhist or Christian—compels one to warp the meaning of other traditions' texts so that they will fit one's own tradition. Exegesis becomes eisegesis . . .

And what is the alternative? It seems to me that the true dialogical hermeneutic must encompass whenever possible both speaking one's personal vision with reference to one's own sources and allowing the vision of others to gain expression based on the sources or their own tradition. Beginning with objective information from both sides, moving on to a reciprocal, productive challenge, and culminating in a mutual transformation (John Cobb). More concretely: proceeding from the obvious divergences between Christianity and Buddhism *in the context of their respective traditions* and looking for points of convergence, for openings, for possibilities of expansion and enrichment.

Masao Abe is of the opinion that this kenotic God, who disintegrates himself in the Absolute Nothingness, not only overcomes Christian monotheism, but also the nihilism of Nietzsche, which he aligns with Relative Nothingness. Why? Because, for Abe, Absolute Nothingness is Absolute Being. And here, by looking at Masao Abe's interpretation of his own Buddhist position, is where new possibilities of understanding are uncovered.

Shunyata—Being—God

Masao Abe brings to his own attention the relationship of shunyata, "Emptiness," and "Being": Being, which is indeed as meagerly objectifiable as it is conceptually graspable, which is not simply a Something, not simply outside of ourselves, is but dynamically identical to our self. Only that "Being" is a primarily positive concept and sunyata, primarily negative. Yet the dialectic, which is characteristic of these "transcendental" concepts (beyond and including all individual things, classifications of being, and categories) may not be overlooked.

The dialectic of Being in western philosophy: the reader might recall that Hegel already has redefined "Being, pure Being—without any further designation" as "pure indeterminateness and vacuity": "There is nothing in it to intuit, if we can speak here of intuiting: or it is only this pure, vacuous intuiting itself. There is little in it to think, or it is equally only this empty thinking. Being, the indeterminate immediate, is indeed nothing, and neither more nor less than nothing." Hegel's subtle dialectic aims at the unity of Being and Nothing: "*pure Being and pure nothing are, then, the same*" ("*Becoming*" in *Wissenschaft der Logik*, ed. G. Lasson, Part I,I, p. 66f).

The reverse of the dialectic of Nothingness in eastern-Buddhist thought! Masao Abe brings attention to this: the "Absolute Nothingness" in a Buddhist sense is not the nihilistic Nothingness. Abe acknowledges the Mahayana teaching that shunyata is non-shunyata and is, therefore, highest shunyata. Although the term shunyata or Emptiness at first sounds negative, it has, according to Abe, a decidedly positive, even religious and soteriological significance: universal and encompassing everything—human, natural, divine—and, precisely so, limitlessly open without any particularly fixed center; dynamically spontaneous and including all opposites (interdependent and reciprocal) within itself: that is Emptiness.

Similarly, Martin Heidegger tried in our time to conceive and express Being in its fullness—not taken to be static and Greek, but, more in the direction of Hegel, dynamic and modern—without being able to put it into a formula. Ever starting anew, he tried to paraphrase Being, to evoke it by allusion: no longer understanding being as isolated from time, as a static condition, but as an occurrence in time, that which is not motionless, abstract, or a mere empty formula, but a happening, establishing, controlling, unhinderedly ordaining, uncovering and concealing, enduring and elusive fullness and liveliness. Being as the all-encompassing and luminating basic happening, which is not effectual by the grace of humanity, but through itself, and carries its meaning in itself. Briefly, Being understood as "Being in becoming."

Are eastern Buddhism and modern western philosophy of Being thereby reconciled at the highest philosophical or even religious level? Here, I believe, is where the question must be theologically sharpened: if one can speak in this manner about Being—as something which again and again reveals itself anew through the Nothingness, if, as in Heidegger, Being can be testified to only by means of almost mystical words and images, divine attributes and metaphors—what distinguishes it from God? More precisely: if *Nothingness,* through which Being reveals itself throughout, is *the veil of Being,* is then the Being which belongs to humans, for whose truth we are set upon the path as wanderers and whose human history fate determines, not indeed *the veil of God?*

Just as the question of *differentiation* poses itself within the framework of the concept of Being for western philosophy, so in Buddhism the same question poses itself in the context of the concept of Emptiness. And Masao Abe makes it welcomely clear that the traditional Buddhist position stands in need of clarification, completion, or correction with respect to two points:

1. It is important—in spite of the mutual pervasions of past and present—to take *history* seriously: its direction with respect to each new arisal.

2. It is important—in spite of all dissolutions of opposites—to maintain the distinction of good and evil and to establish an *ethic.*

Given this, according to Abe, it is important for contemporary Buddhism to set out on a serious and urgent task:

1. How to connect the principle of *free will* with the understanding of Emptiness: how can Emptiness, an undetermined spontaneity, accept a personal God in its unlimited openness? Abe has recourse at this point to the aspect of compassion, which Emptiness exhibits along with an aspect of wisdom: in its emptying of self, sunyata concentrates on this special center of compassion, which in Buddhism is called the promise or vow, which should flow out of every "act" and "deed."

2. How the directions, the linearity of time, which is essential for an understanding of history and which in Buddhism, in comparison with Christianity, Marxism, and even Leninism comes decidedly too abruptly, can be connected with the understanding of Emptiness. Here, also, Abe refers to the aspect of compassion in Emptiness: as matters stand, not all people are enlightened. It is the task of the enlightened ones to help the numerous unenlightened people to attain enlightenment—an obviously endless process which necessitates, however, the progression of history: indeed, no eschatology or teleology of history in the Christian or western sense, yet—within the context of a completely dynamic Emptiness—a realized eschatology and an open theology.

I cannot set forth this solution in detail here; Buddhists themselves must first of all judge whether the synthesis is successful from the Buddhist standpoint. For my part, I would like to throw out one more basic question: what is actually the highest truth, what is the ultimate reality in Buddhism? Is it shunyata for all schools of Buddhism?

38   HANS KÜNG

Shunyata—The Central Concept of Buddhism?

Is it really true, historically true, that, despite significant cultural variations in world Buddhism, from the true primitive Buddhism of the first centuries Emptiness was accepted as ultimate reality, as the ultimate truth, as the Dharma? Shunyata, as it is well known, appears in only a few passages of the Pali canon. That it became the central concept for the Madhyamika which is therefore called the Shunyavada, is a clear indication of a *major paradigm shift in Buddhism.*

Nagarjuna was the one who *conjoined Emptiness to pratītya-samutpāda* and both to the Middle Path, understood now as a critical-dialectical negation of both and all conceptual extremes. For the first time, in the Madhyamika-karika (and this is the genius of Nagarjuna):

What is caused and conditioned,
That is Emptiness;
That is *pratītya-samutpāda;*
And that is the Middle Path.

In the history of paradigm shifts in Buddhism, in this matter of continuity and discontinuity of ideas, we have here an interesting case of a continuity of ideas, but in a radically new configuration (an equation of these four items not found earlier, not even in the *Prajñāpāramitā*).

It is difficult to overlook the fact that in the Buddhist tradition Emptiness is used also in another sense. And this new approach finds expression already in a work formally ascribed (in the broad sense) to Madhyamika, in the *Mahāyāna-Uttaratantra,* composed by a philosopher named Saramati around 250 C.E. (or later). And at the center of his vision is the Supreme Being, "spotless, luminous spirit." Different terms are often used here to characterize the Absolute: "suchness" (*tathatā*), "element of dharma" (*dharmadhātu*), "element of the buddhas" (*buddhadhātu*). In this way, the Yogachara doctrine (whose actual founder is Maitreyanatha, ca. 300 C.E. and Asanga, 4th century), resulted in a new kind of "Buddhology," i.e., a new understanding of the true nature of the Buddhas. Their real nature is identical to the Absolute. They have, apart from their "changing body" (*nirmāṇakāya*), i.e., the form of their earthly appearance, a heavenly mode, the "pleasure body" (*sambhogakāya*), and finally the "doctrinal body" (*dharmakāya*), which is their true essence, identical with the Highest Being.

It would be not only a different paradigm, but a different religion, if with all the discontinuities of a paradigm change we would not see some continuity, if despite all variables we would not have some constants. And what would be a Buddhism without refuge to the Buddha, refuge to the Dharma, refuge to the Sangha? Would it be more than some more or less religious philosophy *à la* late-Heidegger or late-Wittgenstein? Are not all sutras supposed to be "Buddha-vachana," words of the Buddha?

In short: shunyata has also to be seen in the context of the macro-paradigm-changes which I tried to analyze in my book *Christianity and the World Religions*. Not only significant cultural variations, but the epochal change of an "entire constellation of beliefs, values, techniques shared by a given community" (Kuhn, 1970), affects radically the refuge in the Buddha, in the Dharma and in the Sangha, and determines also the notion of Shunyata. If I am not mistaken, Masao Abe did not propose Buddhist Ultimate Reality as all Buddhists would understand the term, but as it is understood in a very specific Buddhist paradigm: in the Madhyamika as interpreted by a specific Zen philosophy.

All this leads now, after this plea for a fair hearing of all Buddhist paradigms, to more constructive elaborations in view of the Buddhist-Christian dialogue.

But there is no stifling the critical question—what is a Buddhist supposed to make of talk about an Ultimate Reality, when each and every thing is "empty" and emptiness is somehow everything. Can we talk concretely, or do we go around in circles? So we come back to what is likely the most difficult point in Buddhist-Christian dialogue, which some see as an unbridged abyss.

Two Buddhist Options with Regard to Ultimate Reality

One of the main difficulties posed again and again by dialogue about the central concepts of Buddhism is that they are interpreted by Buddhists themselves in quite different, indeed diametrically opposite ways. We can see this with nirvana, and now with the concept of Emptiness, which is understood very differently even by the first two great philosophical schools of Mahayana Buddhism. Here, it seems to me, we have especially *two* options to consider, of which Masao Abe primarily considered the first.

The first option: Anyone who wishes to can understand "Emptiness" with Nagarjuna and the Madhyamikas as primarily *negative*. In that case, all the beings and facts of everyday life, seen from a distance, are "empty," because they come into being and pass away, neither exist nor do not exist, and in any case "are" not. Thus all positive statements are impossible, the question of an Ultimate Reality, which is not simply identical with this world of passing phenomena, is false and perfectly useless, a projection, a fiction, an illusion. Where does that leave us?

Well, Masao Abe will probably object: Emptiness may not be all negative. Things come into being and pass away. As such they are empty. As such they are there. Emptiness is Suchness, *tathatā*. But that positive note is, it seems to me, rather weak. And it is no accident that Madhyamika is known as Shunyavada, that Hindus and even Buddhists had charged it—at least with the appearance of—Nihilism. Whatever clever dialectical objection you might have, Madhyamika is tied to what we would call a "mystical philosophy." This is because *prajñā* is said to be nondiscursive and Emptiness is said to be known *ultimately* through intuition—and not just by the dialectical critiques which like Kant's or Hegel's a diligent student can ultimately learn without necessarily intuiting Emptiness.

My question is: If, according to Abe, "Emptiness" may not be understood nihilistically as Nothing, then why is there anything at all, rather than nothing? This is the fundamental philosophical question not only for Leibniz, but also for Heidegger about "the marvel of marvels": "Why is there any Being at all—why not, far rather, Nothing?" In other words, are these beings and facts possibly empty, do they possibly have no being, precisely because they are altogether not their own source but are identical, in varying ways, to the one Absolute? This is the teaching not just of a poor "dualist" Christian theology, but also of the second (later) great Mahayana school of Yogachara, which answered some important questions which the Madhyamika did not answer (e.g., that of the origin of this world of appearances), which was a crucial factor in East Asian (and Tibetan) Buddhism and which even today governs the more "theological" Japanese understanding of the doctrines of original Buddhism.

The second option: Also this is an authentically Buddhist position: anyone who wishes can interpret "emptiness" *positively* with the Yogachara school. In fact, it has been said that Yogachara with its interest in an *ālaya-vijñāna* (storehouse consciousness), often identified with the Ultimate Reality or "Suchness" (*Tathatā*), was precisely such a reaction to the seeming "negativism" of Madhyamika. And it is no accident that there rose a new interest in a *positive* Buddha Nature, that the Sutra of Queen Shrimala (*Shrīmāladevī Sūtra*) specifically identifies an *Ashūnya* (Not-Empty). I am not saying that *ashūnya* negates *shūnya* necessarily. I am only saying that there is more than one way to present the Ultimate

Reality, and that the best way for me is to present it dialectically. And that to say there is God or an *Ādi-Buddha* may hardly contradict Emptiness or *pratītya-samutpāda*. In that case, all beings and facts are forms of expression of the one ineffable Highest Being, which also is real. Now, of course, the question of the one true Ultimate Reality which is obviously more than just this world of conditioned co-arising (*pratītya-samutpāda*), which is rather the spotless, luminous, pure spirit, which constitutes the facts and even the Buddhas as their "element"—stands at the center of attention.

No one will ever get an advocate of Yogachara to call this question useless or even falsely put. No wonder the fusion of the Madhyamika and Yogachara traditions was already under way during the heyday of Yogachara in India, and the "new" (but from the Indian standpoint most ancient) notion of the Absolute prevailed. Because, insofar as they did not fall victim to total skepticism, Nagarjuna's successors made one thing clear: All these negations include an *affirmation*. Denial is not the end but the means of discovering the hidden reality, the transcendent ground of everything and at the same time the true nature of things as the norm for true and false. Nagarjuna's great critic, the Vedanta philosopher Shankara (eighth century), who learned so much from him that he has been called a "crypto-Buddhist," thought it consistent to proceed from the "emptiness" of the world of appearances to the true being of Brahman. Shankara in turn was corrected, as we know, by Ramanuja, who defended a modified nondualism, a differentiated unity of the Absolute and the world which is very near to the classical Christian position. And even though the Buddhists themselves rejected a "Brahman," or "God," the majority in no way flatly objected to a transcendence which is immanent. I think there are Buddhists who accept the term "panentheism," and maybe they would accept also the term proposed by Masaharu Anesaki and Theodore Stcherbatsky: "cosmotheistic" (Stcherbatsky, 1978: 55). All these notions of Buddhist transcendence are not as far away from the Christian concept of Ultimate Reality as many imply.

An Eastern-Western Understanding of God

Maybe also Masao Abe could agree with this vision: *Nirvana, Emptiness, Dharmakaya* do, in fact, *manifest qualities of an Ultimate Reality:* a different dimension within phenomena, a truly religious dimension, true reality. Nirvana, Emptiness, Dharmakaya have, in fact, brought about a twilight of the gods or idols: they have supplanted the Hindu gods

as the supreme authority, yet they have not put any other gods—not even
the Buddha—in their place. Nirvana, Emptiness, and Dharmakaya appear in this sense as parallel terms for the Ultimate Reality. Their function is analogous to that of the term "God." Would it, then, be wholly
impermissible to conclude that what Christians call "God" is present,
under very different names, in Buddhism, insofar as Buddhists do not
refuse, on principle, to admit any positive statements?

What is, according to Christianity, the one infinite reality at the
beginning, in the middle, and at the end of the world and humanity?
Based on what I have developed in *Christianity and the World Religions,*
I would like to attempt to answer in a single complex proposition:

> If God is truly the "Ultimate Reality" then God is *all these
> things in one:*
> *nirvana,* insofar as God is the goal of the way of salvation;
> *Dharma,* insofar as God is the law that shapes the cosmos and
> humanity;
> *Emptiness,* insofar as God forever eludes all affirmative deter-
> minations;
> and the *Primal Buddha,* insofar as God is the origin of every-
> thing that exists.

Discourse about the Ultimate Reality that is not at the same time
discourse about the ineffability of the Ultimate Reality easily turns into
idle talk. Discourse about the Absolute is adequate only so long as it is
conducted in the awareness of the dialectic of gripping and releasing,
speech and speechlessness, language and silence, with utmost discretion
in the face of what is not determined by the factitious "mysteries" of the
theologians, but *is simply the secret heart of this reality.* And actually,
silence before this hidden reality is often the most appropriate demeanor,
a silence which comes from the negation that the East so urgently insists
on and that is not continually being drowned out by the affirmations to
which the West is undoubtedly inclined.

Language, to be sure, is a barrier. Yet language can break down
barriers. Language limits, but it can also remove limits and open the way
to the ever greater mystery, for which Nicholas of Cusa used the term
coincidentia oppositorum, the "synthesis of opposites," *the* distinctive
mark, as it were, of the Ultimate. Could it be that from this point we can
make out a structural similarity between that "Emptiness" which, for

Buddhists, transcends all opposites, and that "pleroma," that infinite "fullness" which embraces all opposites?

How, then, can we try to think adequately about the Ultimate? In such a way, at all events, that it simultaneously transcends and permeates the world and humanity: infinitely far and yet closer to us than we are to ourselves, intangible even though we experience its presence, present even when we experience its absence, affirmative through all negations. An Ultimate that pervades the world and still does not merge with it, that encompasses it but is not identical with it: transcendence in immanence. Every statement about Ultimate Reality would, in this approach, have to pass through the dialectic of negation and affirmation. Every experience of Ultimate Reality would have to survive the ambivalence of nonbeing and being, dark night and bright day.

*   *   *   *   *

Author's Note:

The background of this essay can be found in my book *Christianity and the World Religions. Paths to Dialogue with Islam, Hinduism, and Buddhism* (Doubleday, New York 1986).

Editor's Note:

The section in this essay entitled "From Modern Nihilism to Post-Modern Belief in God" has been copied from the English translation of *Existiert Gott?* (Küng, 1980 ET, see p. 105 below). The remainder of the essay was submitted by Professor Küng in German and has been very kindly and ably translated into English by Farrell D. Graves, Jr., a graduate student at the University of Virginia. Professor Küng has approved the translation.

Buddhist Shūnyatā and the Christian Trinity: The Emerging Holistic Paradigm

Michael von Brück

*P*aradigm shifts are fundamental changes in a cultural pattern. Today we are in the midst of a paradigm shift. It is characterized by the emerging awareness that life is a whole and that terms, or words, cannot convey this wholeness. Words are only fragmented images which usually allow only a fragmented experience. The current paradigm change seeks to overcome fragmentation on all levels of reality, precisely at the moment when the results of fragmentation are becoming disastrous.

Presuming and affirming this concern to offset fragmentation, I shall try in this essay to look back into history in order to find situations, expressions and symbols that might help us understand and promote the present paradigm shift. My approach will be cross-cultural and interreligious, and in four main parts:

First, I will discuss the paradigm shift from Hinayana to Mahayana in the history of Buddhism, and compare it with the emerging paradigm shift in the modern West;

Secondly, because it is only in symbols that we perceive reality creatively, I will examine the symbolic representation of reality with respect to these paradigm shifts;

Thirdly, I will explore two traditional symbols that can provide the needed help to overcome fragmentation and promote the wholeness that is central to the emerging paradigm shift: the Buddhist *Shūnyatā* and the Christian Trinity;

Fourthly, using the symbols of *Shūnyatā* and Trinity, I will offer a holistic image of reality that describes the Whole as interrelatedness and resonance.

Paradigm Shifts

Buddhism

It is difficult, if not impossible, to arrive at a clear picture of the paradigm shift in Buddhism that led to the systems of Hinayana and Mahayana.[1] We are simply unable to reconstruct original Buddhism. Nevertheless, what has emerged as the two great systems—or better, paradigms—is well documented. In order to show how a paradigm shift did take place in Buddhism, I would like to focus on a few points of difference between the two systems.

Hinayana represents a rationalistic paradigm (Conze, 1962: 28ff). The basic attitude is psychological, and the means of investigation are the classical *pramānas* (ways of knowing) which are regarded as more or less valid (Stcherbatsky, 1978: 2:43ff; Conze, 1962: 28). Mahayana, on the other hand, represents a supra-rationalistic paradigm. The basic attitude is metaphysical, or even cosmological, insofar as a universal salvation is the focus of practice. The *pramānas* are not valid concerning ultimate realization, which is attained only by means of a transpersonal intuitive experience (*prajñā*).

In Hinayana one seeks to overcome suffering. In Mahayana one takes on suffering for the sake of all sentient beings (Govinda, 1979: 45). This, essentially, is the difference between the Arhat (the Hinayana ideal) and the Bodhisattva (the Mahayana ideal).

In Hinayana, Stcherbatsky says, we find an ontological pluralism. The independent *dharmas* (the immediate constituents of all reality) are real. They are structured elements of empirical reality that do not have any further cause. Reality *is* the network of phenomena constituted by the mutual conditioning of the *dharmas*. In Mahayana we find, according to Stcherbatsky, a kind of monism, or a *cosmotheistic* model, that transcends any differentiated ontology. Reality is one. Differences are epistemic—based on the way we know reality. While Hinayana explains the basic problem of causality by denying causality and affirming a coordination between the independently existing elements, Mahayana follows the middle way of "neither-nor." One has to transcend the very concept of causality, for it is based on the duality of cause and effect. For the enlightened mind, cause and effect are one. That is why in Hinayana *anitya* (impermanence) is the crucial point, whereas in Mahayana it is *shūnyatā* (emptiness) (Murti, 1960: 86).

These abstract differences lead to more practical and more significant conclusions. In Hinayana, nirvana somehow has an existence apart from the *dharmas*—i.e., from the finite world. This implies a kind of dualism. In Mahayana, nirvana is not at all different from samsara—that is, the phenomenal world: the difference between nirvana and samsara is epistemic, not ontological. Mahayana, therefore, represents a shift from Hinayana toward a holistic paradigm. The basis for this shift is the Mahayanist equation between *pratītyasamutpāda* (the dependent coorigination and interrelatedness of all reality) and *shūnyatā,* which implies the equation between nirvana and samsara.

The Modern West

This sketch of the paradigm shift in Buddhism should be sufficient to illustrate the similarities between it and the paradigm shift in our contemporary world. Since this modern shift is still in process, it escapes full and adequate description. Yet some of its basic qualities can be clearly and profitably focused. They are amazingly similar to the shift from Hinayana to Mahayana.

Some of the most important aspects of the emerging paradigm are the following:
1. science is limited and it itself is becoming aware of its limits;
2. the universe is an interrelated wholeness;
3. the observer plays a crucial part in the process of knowing.

According to the emerging paradigm, "matter" and "consciousness" no longer seem to be essentially different. This opens a new avenue for understanding consciousness. One of the most challenging dimensions of this deeper understanding is the question of whether altered states of consciousness offer us a valid, perhaps more comprehensive, picture of reality. Different levels of consciousness disclose different levels of reality. To limit knowledge only to the products of the rational mind—which is the rationalistic-scientific paradigm that emerged in the seventeenth century and has since dominated Western culture—is nothing else than a form of reductionism, though an extremely successful one from the point of view of technology.

As is evident, the emerging paradigm offers an arena for a dialogue between mysticism and science. David Bohm, speaking as a sober and balanced scientist, claims that if one takes the findings of the new physics to be reliable, one has no justification for a fragmented worldview. Bohm is not claiming that physics can or should prove that the claims of the mystics are true (which is impossible since mysticism and science are working on different levels of reality). Yet, in urging the overcoming of fragmentation, both scientists and mystics are advocating one of the clearest and most important aspects of the emerging paradigm.

The Symbolic Representation of Reality

In order to understand the mystery of reality, we need not only reflection or thought, but vision—the vision of the whole. This, however, is not possible without imagination, the ability to re-create reality in the image of our deepest experience. Without this creative faculty, our mind is only a weak reflection of fleeting sense-impressions. Creative imagination is the motor, the moving power; reason is the steering and restricting faculty, which distinguishes between the potential and the actual, the probable and the possible (Govinda, 1981: 4).

It is in symbols that we perceive reality creatively. The symbol, therefore, is the meeting point of experiencing consciousnesses; it is the place where reality becomes aware of itself, mirrors itself, and injects its own reflection back into the sea of reality. By the power of symbols we share in the creative process of reality.

If we want to understand the wholeness of reality, we have to search for a symbol that re-presents and participates in this wholeness.

In Mahayana Buddhism, especially in the Madhyamika school, the key to understanding reality is the symbol of *shūnyatā*—usually translated into English as Emptiness. *Shūnyatā*, as Buddhists announce and Westerners often fail to hear, has nothing to do with nihilism. Nor is it a concept, for it is not meant to determine anything. *Shūnyatā* is a symbol of non-determination. It does not denote some form of observation but is, rather, the very essence of a specific experience. The experiencer and the experienced become one in a state of mind and state of reality called *shūnyatā*. Because of this oneness and the participatory act of establishing *shūnyatā*, we have to call it a symbol.

One of the most talked about symbols of reality being proposed by modern physicists is David Bohm's *holomovement*. It is much more than a scientific term or definition, for it is not definable. It stands for the mystery of reality that underlies all our possible observations and expressions of reality. Drawing a distinction between the implicate and explicate orders, Bohm states:

To generalize so as to emphasize undivided wholeness, we shall say that what "carries" an implicate order is the *holomovement,* which is an unbroken and undivided totality. In certain cases, we can abstract particular aspects of the holomovement (e.g., light, electrons, sound, etc.), but more generally, all forms of the holomovement merge and are inseparable. Thus, in its totality, the holomovement is not limited in any specifiable way at all. It is not required to conform to any particular order, or to be bounded by any particular measure. Thus, the *holomovement is undefinable and immeasurable* (Bohm, 1981: 151).

Through the powerful symbol of the *holomovement,* therefore, modern science is referring to a reality that is beyond all determination. What we see and know is only the explicate order. The explicate, however, is like a condensation of a vast sea of energy. The explicate is *in* the implicate like the ripple in the ocean or the cloud in the air. Thus, metaphors like air and ocean are used to point to reality that is as it is: undeterminable.

To solve the problem of how the ripple or the cloud can be explained, some scientists speak of a formative principle or a formative energy. Both physicist David Bohm and biologist Rupert Sheldrake suggest a formative energy that might be responsible for the multiplicity on the explicate level. They use the image of a radio that receives its energy from the wall socket. The tiny amount of energy from the radio wave *forms* this vast basic energy (which would correspond with the sea of reality—potentiality on which the ripple is a formation). For Bohm this is how the more subtle implicate energy field acts upon and forms the gross explicate phenomena (Bohm and Sheldrake, 1982: 44). But it is not a form imposed on something from the outside; it is "rather an *ordered and structured inner movement that is essential to what things are*" (Bohm, 1981: 12).

Reality, we can summarize, is a whole and, as such, undifferentiated. It has the principle of formative differentiation in itself. All of this can be expressed or suggested only through symbols.

Another symbol for this same holistic insight into reality is offered by the Madhyamika notion of *shūnyatā.*

Like the philosophical insights of modern physics, the Madhyamika philosophy can be seen as a new interpretation of reality—i.e., different both from Vedantic substantialism and the pluralism of earlier Buddhism (Murti, 1960: 121ff). Though early Buddhism did deny permanence and continuity in the debate on causation, it stressed a coordination of being and becoming of separate *dharmas*. This was a permanent principle and was therefore denied by the Madhyamikas. Nagarjuna, the principal philosopher of the Madhyamika school, insisted on total relativity and therefore criticized all substance-views as well as model-views. He identified *shūnyatā* with *pratītya-samutpāda* (dependent co-origination): all forms were empty—emptiness was all forms.

This means that reality *is*, but is also beyond all possible constructions of our mind. Thinking falls into contradictions when it tries to approach reality as a whole. The real is devoid (*shūnya*) of determinations—that is, it is not accessible to reason. It is—using our rational terms—neither existent nor non-existent. It has to be expressed in symbols.

According to the emerging holistic paradigm, we are part of reality. When consciousness operates and discloses something, there is a change in reality. In other words, *knowledge is a creative act,* epistemologically as well as ontologically (in the final analysis, the two cannot be separated). It is in symbols that such creative or transformative knowledge is available and communicable. Symbols indicate our creative participation in changing reality. But to work this way, symbols have to be reexperienced and reinterpreted according to the present "habit-structure" or "karmic" circumstances or new paradigms. That is why I now want to focus attention on the central symbol of Mahayana Buddhism—*shūnyatā*—and of Christianity—the Trinity.

Shūnyatā and the Trinity

Shūnyatā

The Madhyamika texts use the term *shūnyatā* in two different senses, which have to be distinguished though not separated (Ramanan, 1978: 253ff). First, *shūnyatā* refers to the interrelatedness of reality. Here it has the same meaning as *pratītya-samutpāda* and is primarily a matter of phenomenological observation and interpretation. As we have seen, science, especially the new physics, gives evidence that all phenomenal reality is actually a net of causal connections or total interrelatedness. (Physics is thus contributing to a new ecological paradigm.) Nothing exists independently or can have existence on its own (*svabhāva*). In other words, everything is empty of self-existence—that is, everything is *shūnya*.

Second, *shūnyatā* also refers to a level beyond all phenomenal reality. It points toward the transcendent mystery of reality. It is total *beyondness.* The interrelated whole as sum of all parts is not the Whole. The Whole is of a different quality altogether. All potentialities, as well as all actualities, of reality are not *nirvāṇa* or *shūnyatā,* which is precisely beyond the differentiation into potential and actual, or part and whole. *Tathatā,* nirvana, *shūnyatā* do not mean only interrelatedness, but beyondness.

This quality of beyondness is often forgotten by those who try to relate Buddhism and modern science. Ken Wilber warns against the prevalent mistake of identifying the interrelatedness that physics has discovered with the beyondness expressed by *shūnyatā.* The implicate order is not the Absolute or God. It is just the interrelatedness of phenomenal reality. What religions call "God" is beyond this duality of implication and explication and is devoid of such determinations (Wilber, 1982: 251).

But what about Nagarjuna's famous equation of nirvana and samsara? This identification can be properly understood only on the basis of the fundamental epistemological principle in Madhyamika philosophy —the distinction between a relative viewpoint (*saṃvṛti-satya*) and an absolute standpoint (*paramārtha-satya*). From the relative or phenomenological standpoint, samsara is of course not nirvana. The equation is valid only from the absolute viewpoint that transcends all distinctions. But such an insight is not possible on the basis of rationality alone. No rational argument, therefore, can affirm or deny this point of unity. It requires *prajñā*—insight into reality as it really is, without the limiting and conditioning defilements of the mind.

So, although *shūnyatā* in no way intends to affirm non-existence, it does deny the dogmatic affirmation of or knowledge of existence (Murti, 1960: 97). It denies essentialism. Things in their real nature are devoid of essence (*niḥsvabhāva*). The entities making up the world are related by nature and not just by accident. They are *tathatā,* beyond both transitoriness and immutability. Nagarjuna does not deny reality, he does deny the accessibility of reality to reason (Murti, 1960: 126).

Nagarjuna's insights must be considered a real paradigm shift. He did not simply correct or clarify previous views. Rather, he denied the accessibility of the Real to reason and proved it by his dialectical method. This does not mean that he became an agnostic. He found a different level of knowledge—*prajñā*—that gave an empowering insight and new way of "knowing" reality.

So far, we have only said what *shūnyatā* is not. It is much more difficult to state what it is. To do so adequately is impossible since statements have to obey rationality—and *shūnyatā* by its very nature pierces through the rational level into the beyond. I would like to try to point toward (not describe) the positive nature of *shūnyatā* by quoting an extraordinary and profound statement by D.T. Suzuki:

> It is not the nature of *prajñā* (mystical intuition) to remain in a state of *shūnyatā* (the void) absolutely motionless. It demands of itself that it differentiates itself unlimitedly, and at the same time it desires to remain in itself. This is why *shūnyatā* is said to be a reservoir of infinite possibilities, and not just a state of mere emptiness. Differentiating itself and yet remaining itself undifferentiated, and thus to go on eternally in the work of creation ... we can say that it is creation out of nothing. *Shūnyatā* is not to be conceived statically but dynamically, or better, as at once static and dynamic.[3]

This is probably the deepest insight into reality one can have and express on the basis of Madhyamika—and even on the basis of Christian experience, as I will try to explain later. In transcending the concepts of voidness and fullness, Suzuki unifies them in experience—that is, in the experience of reality as a dynamic pattern, as a uniquely differentiated wholeness.

Shūnyatā is, as Lama Govinda calls it, *plenum-void* (Govinda, 1979: 36). It is the nature of all things, oneness in differentiation. "Differentiation is as much an expression of reality as oneness, and form is as important as emptiness" (Govinda, 1976: 52). *Shūnyatā* is the unified awareness that comprehends and transcends both oneness and differentiation. Govinda therefore translates *shūnyatā,* simply yet appropriately, as *transparency* (Govinda, 1976: 51). This translation fits amazingly well into David Bohm's model of reality: *shūnyatā* is the nature of the holomovement, for the explicate order is transparent to the implicate order and the other way around. The following step may be taken though Bohm himself does not take it since it is beyond the reach of science: Ultimately both orders point toward a transcendent ground and are therefore transparent in a continuous process of "transparentiation," which implies our perspectives or cognitive processes as well.

In Buddhist terms, all this means that nirvana does not add anything to *saṃsāra* but is its very nature; yet on the level of sense-perception and rationality, we do not realize this identity (Murti, 1960: 162). The difference between nirvana and samsara is not ontological; it is, rather, a difference in our way of looking, a change of perception, an *epistemic difference* (Murti, 1960: 163). We must remember, however, that in the final analysis the epistemic process is itself a movement in the Whole, thus *paramārthika* (from an ultimate point of view)—there is not difference at all between the ontological and epistimological realm.

Interestingly, T.R.V. Murti adopts, in a slightly less comprehensive sense, the terminology of David Bohm to describe the Buddhist view of reality, before Bohm formulated the terms. Murti explains that the Absolute is *implicate* in all things:

> The Absolute, it is true, is not known in the way that particular phenomena are known. As their reality, however, it is known as the implicate, the norm of all things. The absolute does not possess any attribute of its own; but its presence can be *indicated* even by an ascribed mark (*samāropāt*) (Murti, 1960: 231f).

Like Bohm's implicate order, the Absolute for Murti is implicate in the explicate order. The Absolute is the Reality of the real (*dharmāṇām dharmatā*). It is the Being of being.

The classical text for this universal viewpoint is *Madhyamika Kārikā* XXV, 9. Stcherbatsky's translation brings out the point most clearly:

> Coordinated here or caused are separate things.
> We call this world phenomenal
> But just the same is called Nirvana,
> When viewed without causality, without Coordination
>   (Stcherbatsky, 1978: 206).

We already referred to Murti's explanation of this text above when we discussed the problem of perception.

A fundamental problem is how to disregard causes and conditions in order to arrive at the Whole. Can the Being of being or the implicate order be, as Murti claims, the Absolute, *shūnyatā?* If the Absolute is the norm of all things, it is not all things. Hence, it is beyond the differentiation between being and the Being of all beings, or between norm and its actualization. Murti's explanation, therefore, does not adequately express

the *beyondness* of *shūnyatā,* which, by virtue of its beyondness, can and
does include the phenomenal world. I am afraid that Murti reverted back
to Vedantic reductionism regarding the relation between the Absolute
and the finite.

If the Reality of the real, as an implicate order, is identified with the
Absolute or *shūnyatā,* we would still be caught in a subtle duality between the Reality of the real (implicate) and the phenomenon as expression of this reality (explicate).

Shūnyatā is not the first of two orders (implicate/explicate)—although this is implied. In the first meaning we quoted above it is *also* the
principle of "???" and in this sense the implicate. But it is more. *Shūnyatā*
must be emptied of all duality. It is beyond differentiation into implicate
and explicate. It is beyondness. It is emptied emptiness. This, of course,
does not mean that it is spatially or temporally beyond phenomena. It
transcends spatiality and temporality in such a way that it includes them.
If this were not so, we would not have a real *advaita* (non-duality), or a
genuine polarity constituting oneness. This, by the way, is the problem
with Shankara's view of the many as *māyā*—that is, as an illusion. He
views the phenomenal many as less real than the Absolute Brahman and
as not taken up into a higher order of dynamic oneness. For this reason,
Shankara has problems intelligibly explaining the relationship between
māyā and *māyin* or between *nirguṇa Brahman* (the formless Absolute)
and the realm of *māyā,* as I have argued elsewhere.

I think that Nagarjuna solves this problem of the relation between
the Absolute and the finite in a much more genuinely *advaita*-way. I
would suggest that for him, *shūnyatā* is a relationship in itself, devoiding
itself constantly of essentiality of substance as it constitutes itself as universal relationship. This interpretation is actually a reflection of Suzuki's
central statement quoted above; we will explore it further below. However we try to conceptualize the non-dual nature of the Absolute, the fact
remains, as Murti reminds us, that we know the Absolute in a non-dual
intuition, *prajñā.* In fact, "It (the Absolute) is this intuition itself"
(Murti, 1960: 236).

An etymological perspective on this problematic nature of *shūnyatā*
can be helpful and revealing. *Shūnyatā* comes from the root √*svi* or √*sva.*
The verb derived from this root is *svayati,* which means "to swell, grow,
increase." As far as I know, Stcherbatsky was the first among recent
scholars to refer to this interesting horizon of meaning (Stcherbatsky,
1978: 206). There is another famous Sanskrit root with the same meaning
"to grow, or increase"—√*bṛh,* from which Brahman, the Hindu word for

the Absolute, is derived. Etymologically, the root meaning of *shūnyatā* and *Brahman* are identical!

Such considerations throw confirmatory light on the interpretation of *shūnyatā* we have been suggesting. *Shūnyatā* is a potential in actuality, an energetic process. *Shūnyatā,* therefore, does not imply that there is no absolute reality, but it does mean that this reality is *not* an essential sameness. It is a process that requires distinctions, i.e., growth.

Similarly, *anātman* (not-self) does not mean that there is nothing ultimate in the human being. It does mean, though, that this ultimate reality is not a static sameness, but growth. Moreover, *anātman* was introduced by the Buddha probably because the *ātman* or "self" concept of Hinduism at that time meant the ego. *Anātman* therefore means ego-lessness. Vedanta's later mystical identification of atman-Brahman developed along very similar lines, but with opposed conceptual expressions (Govinda, 1979: 39).

Of course, different schools of Buddhist philosophy interpreted *shūnyatā* in quite different ways. This is only normal, for *shūnyatā* is more than a defined concept. It is a symbol. It is not possible or necessary to enter into the details of this rather complex history of interpretation.

We can summarize the main content of the symbol of *shūnyatā*. Nagarjuna's Madhyamika philosophy suggests the equation of *shūnyatā* and *pratītya-samutpāda*. This implies two conclusions:

First, reality is a non-dual continuum—that is, the Absolute and the phenomenal are perspectives or aspects, and not separate ontological realms.

Second, this one reality is an interrelated Whole, something like a continuous process or self-movement.

Trinity

The symbol of the Trinity has its roots in a dual experience. On the one hand, persons have experienced the presence of Jesus Christ as incarnate Ultimate Reality. In an overwhelming way, Christ represents to his followers the really Real. On the other hand, there is the experience of this presence as an *empowering* presence; it does not allow persons to be observers but empowers them to rise to a higher level of reality themselves. This is what they have called the Holy Spirit. Since both these experiences convey the Ultimate, they have been interpreted as experiences of God the Father (in Jewish terminology). Hence, we have a Trinitarian pattern and symbolism for the interpretation of Christian experience.

Persons discover the Spirit of God as their innermost being. Dwelling within them, the Spirit of God is not, however, to be confused with the empirical ego, which arranges and usually defiles all psychic and mental faculties. The Spirit raises persons beyond their ego, as He dwelled *in* Christ enabling Him to be *in* the Father and the Father *in* Him. All beings share *in* this oneness as they are one among themselves *in* the Father and Son. I will later urge that this advaitic "in" of John's Gospel is significant for both a proper holistic interpretation of reality, as well as for a clear understanding of *shūnyatā*.

An approach similar to the one we suggested for interpreting *shūnyatā* can help us grasp the depths of Trinitarian symbolism. This approach stresses (1) the interrelatedness of reality and (2) the transcendent mystery beyond reality.

Before applying this approach to the Trinity, we must bear in mind that this two-level framework points up a paradox within all language that tries to express the nature of the Absolute. As Ken Wilber expresses it, God is at the same time and under the same conditions both the *ground* and *goal* of reality (Wilber, 1982: 254ff). Reality might be compared to a ladder of cosmic evolution. The Absolute would be both the highest rung as well as the material out of which the ladder is made, including its formative pattern. The Absolute or God would be both the highest level of reality (goal) and the true nature of every level of reality (ground). In the strictest sense, this is a paradox.

In Buddhism, a similar paradox occurs in trying to understand the Buddha-nature. Already and all the time, we *are* the Buddha-nature, and yet we have to *realize* it through practice. This was Dogen Zenji's great problem of original enlightenment (*hongaku*) and acquired enlightenment (*shikaku*); Dogen finally solved it in a practice based on original enlightenment (*Shōbōgenzō, "Bendōwa"*).

For reason alone, this unity is difficult to grasp, yet it is clearly experienced when in actual practice the ego-subject is overcome and filled by *the* Subject (God, Buddha-nature, Christ in us, the Spirit): my spirit is taken up into the Holy Spirit, and the Holy Spirit reflects and merges into my spirit. The two become totally united, but according to Christian experience, they do not become a lifeless identity. This *unifying process in* the Spirit *through* the Son *toward* the Father is the Christian Trinitarian experience. It is what Christians could call enlightenment as a process of participating in the Divine.

First of all, the Trinity means *the interrelatedness of reality*. What is implicate in the Father becomes explicate in the Son and unites in a process of creative resonance in the Spirit. Insofar as God is the ground of the universe, this Trinitarian pattern expresses the dynamic oneness in diversity or *advaita* (non-duality) of individuation and unification expressed and manifested on *all* levels of reality. It mirrors also the spiritual path that is the realization of the return to the source in a transformation of being. God is above (*epi*), through (*dia*) and in (*en*) all (Eph 4:6) in a *perichoretic union.*

Perichōrēsis is the dance, the continuum of self-movement or the dynamic self-existence of this interrelated Triuneness. John of Damascus finds this metaphor a most appropriate description of the threefold inter-relatedness within Divinity (*De Fide Orthodoxa,* PG 789-1228). God is not a monistic principle, but a differentiating unity—therefore, always differentiated as a continuum of oneness. What we experience as the phenomenal or created world participates in the divine interrelatedness, i.e., in God's knowledge and love.

The way *to* or *from* the source *through* the transformation of the individuated reality *in* participating in the mystery of the divine dance can perhaps be illustrated like this:

TO/FROM

(Father, Source, Ground)

THROUGH   IN

(Son, personal trust)   (Spirit, mystical participation)

Each moment of the process implies the other two. The three persons of the Trinity relate to each other in perfect *kenōsis.* Each empties itself into the other. The symbol of the *cross* is actually the expression of the inner relationship of the Trinity. Each person *is* only insofar as it is relationship and self-emptying.

This relational oneness is most clearly experienced in love and knowledge, both of which depend on the merging of two into one consciousness without collapsing into identity. Consciousness becomes aware of itself only when it realizes what it is conscious of. Although it is unified in itself, it is so only on the basis of a distinction. Even pure consciousness, insofar as it is awareness, has this dynamic, relational aspect.

This is also the case when two consciousnesses meet and share each other in a perfect union of synchronized and united activities. They are individuated *and* include each other not only as the other's object, but as subjects of each other's identity. This relationship is realized and felt in deep experiences of prayer and meditation, as Beatrice Bruteau has convincingly shown. She observes that "this entering into, and sharing the consciousness of, another self is the most characteristic act of a self. Dualism has passed over into nondualism, by the very intensity of its own dualistic energy. By desiring the other more and more, one has obliged ultimately to enter into the very life of the other" (Bruteau, 1983: 306). It is an entering into the other's rhythmic pattern, a being in phase with him/her, as it were, a real *perichōrēsis*. Dr. Bruteau also applies this pattern of contemplative prayer to the rhythmic unity of the Trinity in order to explain Trinitarian distinctions:

> This distinction arises from the existential reality of the autonomous acts of knowing and loving which also constitute the unity. So the plurality and the unity are both referred to the same act, and that act is characteristic of the highest conscious selfhood. If Ultimate Reality is of the nature of selfhood, it must be a complex unity of this sort. . . . This distinction is not due to a distance between Creator and creature, but is the same kind of distinction that prevails inside the Godhead itself (Bruteau, 1983: 309).

If, then, the Trinity is first of all the interrelatedness of reality, then, secondly, this inexpressible inner-Trinitarian relationship is also a *transphenomenal unity which includes the explicate manifestation.* As this unity it is always beyond any possible phenomenal state, since the phenomenal would be defined by what it is not. First we saw that the Trinity is the ground of reality (the material out of which the ladder is made). Now we see the second point: the Trinity as the goal of the universe (the highest rung). Whatever reality is, it is not yet what it is, because the Trinitarian perichoretic movement is creativity. The explication of the source in the incarnate Son and its reinjection into the ground through the Spirit is an evolution or graded manifestation of awareness. It is the realization of the Trinitarian *perichōrēsis.* The Trinity is the very nature (or pattern) of consciousness that realizes reality is not outside reality but is the highest level of reality itself. Because this is so, any conscious act is a self-realization of reality. It is a manifestation of the ground of Being that explicates being as a creative insight into itself. This, then, is why spiritual awareness, as achieved by individuals and by humankind in general, is of utmost importance: it is a participation in the divine dynamism. As Paul Tillich maintains, the nature of such participation of the creature in Trinitarian life can be understood only in some kind of non-dual model or context (Tillich, 1969: 70ff). To participate implies both identity and non-identity. A part of the whole is not identical with the whole, and yet the whole cannot be what it is without the part. Tillich, therefore, attempts to think not in terms of substances but of dynamic being that is shared by all individuals (Tillich, 1969: 73). The identity implied in participation is grounded in this dynamism of being. In this way, the dynamism of the individual is a realization of the dynamism of all that is not this individual, and vice versa. This is exactly what the *perichōrēsis* of the Trinity expresses. The complexity of reality *is* the divine dynamism in a continuous process of unification; and this process is constituted by the power of consciousness.

I can summarize these remarks on the non-duality of the Trinity[4] by pointing out three basic insights that the Trinitarian symbol seeks to express:

1. The Ultimate is at the same time both *beyond* as well as *in* all experiences. The realization of this paradox depends on the intensity of one's awareness of or participation in God. The Absolute is *in* all experiences because there is nothing that is not an explication or manifestation of what we call the Absolute. It is *beyond* any possible experience since, as the goal of all reality, it transcends both the conditioned and the unconditioned, and all other possible dualities that make up experience. The Absolute is never the sum of all partialities but the unification of part and whole in a dynamic process.

2. The Ultimate is expressed in and through all material as well as spiritual processes. The Unity of the Trinity suggests a non-dualistic relationship of *sistence* (Father), *ek-sistence* (Son), and *in-sistence* (Spirit); this threefold divine process integrates all partial processes occurring on different levels of reality. Since the ground of reality is self or consciousness, we can infer that all manifested reality shares in this quality of the ground, of course in different degrees. Any dualism between matter and spirit therefore becomes meaningless. We should instead see reality as a graded manifestation of consciousness. The degree of interaction between "parts" or "individuals"—that is, the degree of "being-one-in-another"—marks the degree of realization of consciousness.

3. The Ultimate can be known through the act of participating in its

very nature. This nature is *perichōrēsis*—that is, union in diversity, or the process of unfication of complexities. *In* this process, the Godhead has its oneness. Godhead, therefore, is beyond time; it never collapses into a motionless sameness. Different beings participate in different ways and degrees in the Trinitarian movement—that is, they are on different levels of realization of their true nature. Their true nature is kenotic—a process of constant self-emptying and being filled by other beings. As finite beings become aware of their true nature, they tune into the Trinitarian dance or resonate with the dynamic nature of the Trinity.

Reality as Interrelatedness or Resonance

Shūnyatā and Trinity

To relate, as we have done, the emerging holistic paradigm to the symbols of *shūnyatā* and Trinity is to explore more clearly and more challengingly the meaning of what is presently going on in the spiritual history of humanity. The multidimensional symbols of *shūnyatā* and *Trinity,* if properly interpreted and communicated, can work as powerful agents in overcoming the fragmentation that threatens our modern world.

The modern situation calls for a cross-cultural effort to grasp and live the meaning of *shūnyatā* and Trinity. We might say, using a simile from acoustics, that the two symbols *resonate* with each other. We can imagine our effort to relate *shūnyatā* and Trinity as a matter of placing one symbol in the vibration range of the other and of observing its resonance. The resonance pattern will enable us to know the specific kind of interrelationship we are exploring. This image of resonance is not merely a personal whim or preference of mine; it is a key symbol used by Dogen Zenji to express the meaning of *shūnyatā*—i.e., the interrelatedness and transcendence of Reality.

We have already heard Suzuki's extraordinary statement on the nature of the experience of *prajñā*—that is, the experience of Ultimate Truth. He stated that *shūnyatā* remains in itself, though in a process of differentiation. *Shūnyatā* is the reservoir of infinite complexity comprehending all actual and possible manifestations. Therefore, it creates out of nothing in a process of differentiation, while remaining beyond differentiation. Beyond the distinction of static and dynamic, it includes both. *Shūnyatā* therefore can be termed both static and dynamic, one and multiple—or *perichōrēsis.*

I cannot imagine a more profound philosophical interpretation of the Trinity. The Trinity is this reservoir of infinite possibilities, differentiating itself eternally in three persons, and yet remaining one. It is a differentiated oneness—not monism, but *advaita*. *Advaita* is a category transcending logical distinctions, therefore out of the reach of concepts and neat definitions. So we have to create paradoxes in order to point toward *tathatā* or to express the experience of participating in the Trinity. The Bible and Christian mystical literature are full of such paradoxes, and in Zen Buddhism they are deliberately used as propaedeutical aids.

Using John Damascene's image of the dance (*perichōrēsis*) again, we can acquire a feeling for what these symbols convey. The dance is a dance only insofar as it retains the same structure or form. But this oneness or sameness is differentiated. It brings forth differences constantly, in the creativity of its movement. The dance is a totally interrelated wholeness. In other words, each movement of the dance has its meaning and form only insofar as it realizes itself in the continuous explication of the different "steps."

In later Buddhist philosophy, the dynamic, mutually interrelating aspect of *shūnyatā* was beautifully extolled by Dogen Zenji (1200–1252), especially in his investigations into Buddha-nature (Sanskrit: *buddhatā;* Japanese: *busshō*) (Kim, 1980: 160ff). In Dogen's time, Buddha-nature was understood as some kind of potentiality for sentient beings in the six realms. Dogen had to modify this view when he discovered that *busshō* is absolute inclusiveness for all beings or for whatever is generated by the functional interdependence of conditions and forms in the universe. In this way, Dogen overcame an anthropocentric or biocentric viewpoint, and avoided the implication of a subtle dualism of actuality and potentiality.

Buddha-nature is therefore not a receptacle that contains everything. Each form, rather, is perfect in its suchness and in no need of being contained in anything else. Really, then, *tathatā* (suchness) is identical with *buddhatā* (Buddha-nature). Dogen could say that all sentient beings are the true body of the entire universe (*Shōbōgenzō*, "Sengai-yuishin"). In this view, the Buddha-nature is not permanence as opposed to an impermanent world of forms. In transcending each existence, the Buddha-nature bears the negative within itself. This aspect of the non-existence of the Buddha-nature (*mu-busshō*) is not an antithesis to existence, but one of the poles in a non-dualistic structure. It points to the "liberating and transcending powers inherent in the Buddha-nature which liberate fixation and the particularities of existence" (Kim, 1980: 169).

Dogen's *mu-busshō* recognizes a dynamism in the Ultimate that expresses an experience similar to that which a Christian might call *kenōsis* or the Cross. It is an intuitive experience of personhood that realizes that one gains one's identity by totally devoiding or desubstantializing oneself onto the other. This is the mystery of love!

Furthermore, "The Buddha-nature actualizes itself not in such ways as from potentiality to actuality, from the not-yet to the already, from the lower to the higher, from the hidden to the manifest, but coeval and coessential with what persons act out in their activities and expressions" (Kim, 1980: 179).

In Christian terms this is the experience of the *anthropos pneumatikos,* the spiritual person, whose spirit resonates with and in the Spirit of God (as opposed to the *anthropos psychikos,* the ego-centered person) (1 Cor 2:14; 15:44, 46; Jude 19). This resonance in the Spirit is a unification not only of wills but also, and especially, of awarenesses, a unity that transforms one's whole being. One becomes aware of a primary and cosmic truth—that *love,* as symbolized in the innertrinitarian relationship, is the ultimate nature of Reality.

When God's Spirit works in us and is united with our spirit, and when our spirit is tuned to God's presence, we know. We resonate. This is another way of saying, as Nicholas of Cusa says of God, that Reality is *coincidentia oppositorum.* It is an attempt to think wholeness which Hinduism, Buddhism and Christianity cannot neglect.

To experience and describe reality as both static and dynamic, as does Suzuki, is part of the original core of Buddhism. The early Yogacharins tried to divide the *Dharmakāya*—their symbol for Ultimate Reality—into a polarity that would express its simultaneously static and dynamic character—that is, its *svabhāvakāya* ("essential body") and its *jñāna-kāya* ("wisdom body"). According to Stcherbatsky, "the first is the motionless (*nitya*) substance of the universe, the second is *anitya*—that is, changing, living" (Stcherbatsky, 1978: 2:195, n. 3). Both are *Dharmakāya.* Change and the unchangeable are one.

The polar dynamism that the Yogachara and other schools of Buddhism find in the Ultimate is also contained, perhaps even more emphatically, in Nagarjuna's equation of *pratītya-samutpāda* and *shūnyatā.* This equation of Emptiness and process, as proposed by Nagarjuna, Dogen, Suzuki, and others, comes much closer to the Trinitarian *perichōrēsis* than does the much discussed Mahayana theory of *Trikāya* or the "Three Bodies."

The three bodies designate different aspects or "levels of appearance" (or "manifestations") of the Absolute Reality. What "levels of appearance" actually means is subject to controversy in different Buddhist schools. *Dharmakāya* (the body of *dharma*) is without any attributes. It is a oneness comprising everything which all Buddhas have in common. It is absolute beyondness. *Saṃbhogakāya* (the body of enjoyment) is a subtle realm which can be experienced spiritually. The different Buddhas of meditation have different qualities refering to different aspects of this subtle reality. *Nirmāṇakāya* (the body of manifest being) refers to the historical Buddhas who appear in physical form. Gautama Shakyamuni was one of them. They are incarnations of the Absolute.

The Trikaya doctrine has often been compared to the Trinity; the comparison is warranted insofar as *Trikāya* points to the undivided wholeness that is manifesting itself on all three levels of reality or, better, that is constituting all levels of reality through its self-manifestation. *Shūnyatā,* however, is a more basic, far-reaching symbol and therefore more appropriately compared to the Trinity, for it expresses not only the manifest aspect of the Absolute (something like the economical Trinity), but the very *nature* of Reality as interrelatedness in itself (the immanent Trinity).[5]

Lama Govinda strongly affirms this coinherence of finite and Infinite, one and many. He maintains that individuation (what perhaps can be called the formative principle) is just as important as universal oneness. For him, individuality is one of the focal points of the universe. It is not confined to limits, but "is rather a focal point of radiation which contains the whole universe" (Govinda, 1979: 30). Therefore, individuality is not contradictory to universality, nor is plurality to oneness. Such a view does not exclude a hierarchical interpretation of the Trikaya doctrine (establishing oneness across different levels), but it does affirm the holoarchic model (establishing total interrelatedness within each level) as equally valid. All concepts have to be transcended. Even *shūnyatā* and nirvana as concepts, models, or symbols are open and "allow us to proceed," as Govinda says. They invite us to participate in emptying emptiness or in sharing in perichoretic love.

This perichoretic love is a continuous integrating of all levels of reality into the Whole. The Whole is, as it were, continuously being built up. Refusal to integrate or to resonate in the rhythm of this unity-in-distinction is what one can call sin. Sin is based on inertia or ignorance. Both are forces of separation.

The emerging paradigm we have been discussing seeks to overcome this history and continued threat of fragmentation. Whether it will succeed or not is the question that frightens and challenges our present generation. A necessary condition for overcoming separation and for building a new, united world is that more and more people tune into and work with Reality as it really is—Reality as differentiated oneness or as the *shūnyatā* of the Trinity or the Trinity of *shūnyatā*. To tune to Reality is to live and promote the dynamism of unity and complexity that mark "the way things are," or as Dogen wrote about the One and the many:

Though not identical, they are not different.
Though not different, they are not one;
Though not one, they are not many (Kim, 1980: 164).

Holomovement and Creativity

Within the emerging holistic paradigm, David Bohm, Rupert Sheldrake, and others are very concerned about the question of creativity. Just what is the "power" or energy that accounts for the irregular, the novel, the never-before seen or deemed—and for the new and transcausal (or trans-karmic) freedom that bounds beyond the limits of the given?

We must, I think, assume a transcendent suchness that is neither form nor formlessness but both. What makes reality a continuum and gives it its unity is this "orderly series of stages of enfoldment and unfoldment" that cannot be localized but penetrates all that we call space (Bohm, 1981: 184). Bohm explains the continuity of existence as a very rapid recurrence of similar forms, very much like a rapidly spinning bicycle wheel that gives the impression of a solid disc rather than of a sequence of rotating spokes, which would be separate entities (Bohm, 1981: 183). This image comes very close, of course, to the Buddhist intuition of interdependent origination or *dharma* factors. It sees continuity and sameness in a dynamic pattern of relationship, much like the Trinity (the three persons are not separate entities either). A similarity of order is preserved *in* the pattern of the unfolding-enfolding movement. This is also how consciousness works. It is not a mere tuning into the past (memory), nor anticipation of possibilities, but a direct resonance with what is going on on all levels of movement. Since there is no duality, we can describe consciousness as reality and reality as consciousness.

The recognition of an underlying continuity or unity is also found in the Buddhist notion of impermanence (*anitya*). According to the *anitya* doctrine, origination and decay are simultaneous happenings of one movement. They are aspects. There is no continuity without change. But neither is there change that does not repeat the subtle pattern of interrelated wholeness. As the new physics tells us, you cannot observe a particle without changing it—that is, without changing finally the entire universe, for each particle is related to all other particles. But this change of the universe is not chaotic; rather, it responds to an *ordered* underlying structure and form.

For Dogen, time is the absolute now (*nikon*), realizing past, present, and future in a single event of awareness. Mutual identity of existences and mutual interpenetration (*sosokusonyū*) is his formula for affirming simultaneity as the central expression of the Buddha-nature, which is the actuality of the present. The "present" is not a piled-up past but the awareness of *all* time (*Shōbōgenzō*, "Uji"). " 'Continuity' in this view is not so much the matter of a succession or contiguity of inter-epochal wholes as that of the *dynamic experience of an intra-epochal whole of the absolute now* in which the selective memory of the past and the projected anticipation of the future are subjectively appropriated in a unique manner" (Kim, 1980: 208ff). Continuity is the dynamism of multi-dimensional time that moves "horizontally" as well as "vertically" (*Shōbōgenzō*, "Uji"). From the perspective of the Ultimate, according to Dogen, there is not evolution but *perichōrēsis* (if we may use a Christian term).

According to both Dogen and Bohm, reality can be seen as a resonance pattern within the phases of unfoldment-enfoldment. I would like to suggest that these "phases" can be interpreted, symbolically, as the "perichoretic steps": Father, Son, and Spirit.

Father	Son	Spirit
(Implicate)	(Explicate)	(Integration)

The Whole is the movement of integration, the "dancing" wholeness that is never integrated but is in the *process* of integrating itself. From this perspective, I suggest that what Bohm is trying to express with his image of "undivided wholeness" might be more aptly indicated by "integrating wholeness."

The interrelatedness between implicate and explicate in the actuality of resonance allows an infinite interaction; and this is what we can call *creativity.* New wholes are generated constantly on all levels of reality. Both Bohm's notion of implicate intelligence and Sheldrake's proposal for "morphic resonance" (Bohm and Sheldrake, 1982: 47) (or a process of learning that allows change of habit) try to image the regeneration constantly taking place in the creative interplay between explicate and implicate orders (and the transcendent ground/goal). The mutual ejection and injection releases creative impulses that take shape in new, concrete acts/events/things/thoughts.

Creativity and stability constitute a polarity. It is necessary to have both openness toward the beyond and relatively fixed forms (the past). The polarity pivots on the need for each generated or ejected thing to become a no-thing again—that is, to be injected once more into the implicate order or the ground. Otherwise, the process bogs down because of inertia, a counter-tendency opposed to creativity; we are talking about sin, or non-response, or non-resonance. The importance of the Cross, what gives it universal significance, is that it points up the necessity and value of becoming a no-thing. The cross symbolizes the devoiding or transcending turn into the other and finally into the Whole.

The Whole is devoid (*shūnyatā*) of determination. There are no "knots" in the Trinitarian net (this would be tritheism). The Whole is more than and cannot be reduced to the evolutionary process, yet the Whole contains an evolutive phase. The phases are beyond any of the orders but are reflected in all possible orders. Thus, the Father is not the implicate order but is manifest in all orders. Likewise with the other persons of the Trinity.

Reality is a process of "differentiating itself and yet remaining in itself undifferentiated" (Suzuki). This is what Buddhism calls *shūnyatā* and what Christianity experiences as the Trinity. We participate totally in this dynamism, which is the Ultimate, God. We are eternally merging into God and God into us, but we are never sucked up into an undifferentiated identity.

We might envision this paradoxical unity of differentiation and undifferentiation as a symphony that unfolds in continuous resonance with itself across and beyond time. The whole is there in each part, but it unfolds in time. Each particular note has its specific meaning and quality from the implicate structure of the whole, and the whole simultaneously *in* as well as *beyond* each musical phrase. A genius (like Mozart, as it has been reported) can hear the whole directly in an intuitive perception beyond the time-bound sequence. And yet, time is contained in the whole; it is implicate. The whole resonates in the parts; and the parts' suchness is to resonate as the whole. It is the same with dance, and that is why the Trinitarian *perichōrēsis* is such a profound model.

Conclusion

The emerging holistic paradigm seeks to overcome fragmentation. This is its existential concern, one which, today, is vitally important. What I have tried to show is that this new paradigm, with its concerns, has deep, ancient roots. Our creative task is to regenerate the old so as to build the new more soundly and promisingly.

According to Christianity and, if my analysis of *shūnyatā* is valid, according to at least some schools of Buddhism, the deepest, final experience of humankind does not point toward a motionless substance, but toward *creative participation* in the *plenum-void,* which is *resonance* and therefore *perichōrēsis* or *shūnyatā.*

Notes

1. *Editor's note:* Von Brück is here adopting the Mahayana view of Buddhist history. The reader should clearly understand that, despite some superficial similarities, Hinayana cannot be identified with Theravada. Hinayana is an extinct form of Buddhism to which Mahayana sees itself as a correction. Theravada is a living system which continues independently of Mahayana.
2. Two particles separated in space influence each other's spin. If there were a connection understood in the usual terms of causality, the signal would travel faster than the speed of light which Einstein rejected. Hence, the particle seems to "know" what the other one is doing simultaneously. They might refer to a "common ground."
3. D.T. Suzuki, *Essays in East-West Philosophy,* Charles A. Moore, ed. (Honolulu, 1951), as quoted by W.T. Stace, *Mysticism and Philosophy* (London: Macmillan, 1961), pp. 176ff.
4. For a detailed study of the *advaita* of the Trinity, see Michael von Brück, *Advaita und Trinitaet: Indische und christliche Gotteserfahrung im Dialog der Religionen* (unpublished *Habilitation-thesis,* Rostock University, 1980); idem, "Advaita and Trinity: Reflections on the Vedantic and Christian Experience of God with Reference to Buddhist-Non-Dualism," *Indian Theological Studies,* Vol XX (1983) 37–60.
5. The problem with the Trikaya is that either *Dharmakāya* or even a higher or more abstract principle is often considered to be *tathatā* or *shūnyatā.* But this is questionable since according to Suzuki's interpretation of *shūnyatā,* reality in its interplay within the Trikaya should be suchness and nothing else. Otherwise, the door is open to a new form of dualism, a problem not seen clearly enough by Murti (1980: 284ff).

Buddhist Shūnyatā and the Christian Trinity: A Response to Michael von Brück

Paul O. Ingram

*M*ichael von Brück's essay, "Buddhist Shūnyatā and the Christian Trinity: The Emerging Holistic Paradigm," is a brave attempt to focus Buddhist-Christian dialogue on what he calls "the new paradigm shift" in Buddhist and Christian faith. He believes this paradigm shift is best illustrated by the Mahayana Buddhist doctrine of Emptiness (*shūnyatā*) and the Christian doctrine of the Trinity. He proposes treating these teachings (1) as complementary Buddhist and Christian symbols that unlock the nature of this new paradigm shift, and (2) as symbols invoking paradigm shifts comparable with the paradigm shift he sees emerging within modern scientific theory, particularly relativity theory, quantum physics, and the principle on uncertainty, so that (3) he can show how and why *shūnyatā* and the Trinity are complementary symbols which, if conjoined together, "offer a holistic image of reality that describes the Whole as interrelatedness and resonance."

I substantially agree with von Brück's conclusions—as far as I can understand them—mostly because they support the general thrust of my own work in Buddhist-Christian dialogue. However, my general agreement is also the source of serious uneasiness about this essay. In my opinion, it fails on two grounds: linguistic and historical. Accordingly, I will limit my response to these two problem areas.

The Linguistic Problem

The primary difficulties of this essay originate in von Brück's assumptions about the function of language. Specifically, he uncritically assumes that language *always* falsifies human experience of reality, meaning "the way things really are," because language always entails a dualistic world view that separates us from the reality we experience. But, he believes, the goal of Buddhist religious practice and Christian mystical discipline is to apprehend reality "as it is" prior to all verbalization about what reality is. Presumably, only Buddhas and Christian mystics, even perhaps mystics in other religious Ways, know that all talk about reality is "secondary order truth." Only they know how to establish valid symbolic relationships with reality that, while *involving* language, are not *of* language. If I have accurately understood von Brück's assumptions about language, then it appears to me that he tries to establish his conclusions on some rather amazing contradictions. For the sake of brevity, I will only point to three.

First, his assumptions about the nature and function of language are not supported by modern linguistic theory, by contemporary philosophy of language, by the Buddhist authorities he cites, by the writings of most Christian mystics, or by modern philosophy of science. The question is, how is it possible to have a non-linguistic understanding of reality, when the primary means by which human beings have any sense of reality is linguistically constructed? Buddhists achieve the sorts of meditative experience that Buddhist doctrine leads them to *expect* to experience. Christians experience reality according to the way Christian teaching *trains* them to experience reality, just as the working experience of natural scientists is guided by whatever scientific paradigms guide their research. On what epistemological grounds does von Brück so radically separate theory (*theōria*) from practice (*praxis*)?

My point is not that we are completely locked into our particular linguistically constructed frames of reference. If we were, dialogue between Buddhists and Christians would be impossible. But *that* we must existentially, culturally, and socially dwell within *some* language system, some linguistic frame of reference, is the absolute precondition for having any meaningful sense of "the way things really are" that is distinctively human. We can never escape language, even if we are Buddhas or Christian mystics or scientists. As the biography of Helen Keller so graphically demonstrates, without language a human being's sense of reality is no different than, say, a dog's. True, dogs and humans may share similar relationships to trees. Indeed, most of us have done so on occasion. But human beings can sense the beauty of trees, enjoy poetry about trees, interpret trees as religious symbols, build houses out of trees, plant trees, or try to preserve forests of trees—precisely because, unlike dogs, human beings are language-using beings. Our sense of reality is always a derivative of language. Language does not separate us from reality; language creates whatever sense of reality human beings are able to possess.

Secondly, language is also the chief means by which human beings falsify reality. Here lies the half-truth of von Brück's interpretation of the role of language in Buddhist and Christian experience. But no Buddhist teacher (with the possible exception of D.T. Suzuki), Christian mystic, or scientist ever seriously believed that language can or should be abandoned in order to experience reality "as it is" prior to language. Our choice is never between language or reality, but between "enlightened" and "unenlightened" use of language in our struggle for a sense about how "things really are." "When you see a Buddha, kill a Buddha," is a collection of words arranged in a sentence according to rules of syntax and grammar. The words of this sentence express meanings pointing beyond the literal definitions of the words of this sentence. But all meaning disappears without the words arranged in a particular syntactical pattern. Thus, Christian mystics wrote about their experiences in language they intended to be suitable for communicating the meaning of their experiences, to themselves and to others. We do not know anything, as human beings, until we set it out in some linguistic interpretation, whether this be in a short story, a play, a novel, a poem, a riddle, a joke, a treatise, a doctrine, a theological system, a scripture, or a *kōan.*

So truth and falsehood, enlightenment and delusion, are possible precisely because we are linguistic beings. If this is true, then all language must be symbolic, pointing beyond itself to realities which nevertheless cannot be reduced to linguistic formulae. In other words, paradigms, metaphors, similes—all carry symbolic meanings because language itself *is* symbolic. Always, at all times, it seems to me, our relation to reality, whether a truthful relation or a false relation, is symbolic.

Thirdly, if what I have asserted—admittedly without sufficient argumentation—adequately describes how we construct and apprehend reality, or what we hope or imagine reality might be, then an important fact is overlooked by von Brück. Just because we cannot say *everything* there is to say about reality does not mean we can say nothing, even if we are not Buddhas or mystics or scientists. Our option is not to experience reality prior to any verbalization about reality, for this is not possible.

Our option is the "enlightened" or "unenlightened" use of language.
Even the Buddhas talked. And if von Brück's assumptions about language are true, then his essay is incoherent; he uses language to write
about the impossibility of using language to apprehend "the way things
really are"—surely a very odd methodological position in which to be,
since it is very difficult to write about paradigm shifts in Buddhism and
Christianity without using language.

The Historical Problem

The second difficulty I have with von Brück's essay is his uncritical
disassociation of ideas from their historical contexts. I mean by this
observation that he forces his perceptions of emerging paradigm shifts
onto Buddhism and Christianity in an ahistorical way that neither tradition can support. In the process, he unintentionally misrepresents both
religious Ways, which in turn pulls the methodological rug out from
under Buddhist-Christian dialogue.

There may indeed be "holistic" paradigms emerging in modern
Buddhist and Christian experience that correlate with the world as perceived through the paradigms of the natural sciences. If so, these paradigm shifts are expressions of the histories of Buddhist and Christian faith
and experience, and one needs to specify carefully what these historical
connections are. Otherwise, ideas are imposed on Buddhist and Christian
encounter that are foreign to Buddhist and Christian persons participating in the dialogue.

Perhaps I can illustrate the problem by von Brück's treatment of
Nagarjuna's notion of *shūnyatā* and his comparison of the Buddhist
trikāya doctrine with the Christian doctrine of the Trinity.

The question is: what did Nagarjuna mean when he taught that all
things and events, including his own views, are "empty"? Von Brück's
first error is that he based much of his analysis of Nagarjuna's conception
of Emptiness on T.R.V. Murti's book, *The Central Philosophy of Buddhism*. The problem with following Murti's interpretation of Buddhist
thought, and especially the Madhyamika tradition, is that his analysis
rather uncritically transformed Buddhist thought into an inferior sort of
Upanishadic philosophy. Murti, in other words, read Madhyamika tradition through the philosophical assumptions of Advaita Vedanta—thus,
in my opinion, completely misrepresenting Nagarjuna and the Madhyamika. Murti really did not believe that the Buddha and early Buddhist
philosophers actually taught the theory of causation named "dependent

co-origination" (*pratītya-samutpāda*). Accordingly, Murti falsified Nagarjuna's thought, and this falsification extended to his analysis of Madhyamika and Mahayana philosophy in general. Likewise, in following Murti's work too closely, von Brück incorporates Murti's distortions into his own analysis of the notion of Emptiness, which in turn places his conclusions about emerging paradigm shifts in Buddhism and Christianity on rather shaky grounds.

There are better English sources than Murti's work for unlocking the meaning of Nagarjuna's teachings. In my opinion, the best of these is Frederick J. Streng's study, *Emptiness, A Study in Religious Meaning.* The following summary of what I take to be the meaning of the Buddhist doctrine of Emptiness is based largely on Streng's work. I offer this summation not because I wish to undercut von Brück's analysis and conclusions, but because I think a more accurate historical understanding of Nagarjuna's thought supports his conclusions.

First of all, Nagarjuna did not employ the notion of Emptiness to establish the superiority of his own philosophical viewpoint over against other viewpoints. He was not interested in establishing his own philosophical viewpoint at all, but in demonstrating the epistemological incoherency of all philosophical viewpoints, including Buddhist viewpoints and his own views of Buddhist viewpoints.

The whole point of Nagarjuna's concept of Emptiness is that all things and events, including all philosophical points of view about things and events, are "empty" of "own-being" (*svabhāva*). Because all things and events are empty, therefore, all things and events are impermanent. Accordingly, if we experience everything as empty of "own-being," including our philosophical-religious doctrines, we cease clinging (*upādāna*) to them, because in an impermanent universe, there is nothing to which I can cling. And when we stop clinging, we cease experiencing life as unsatisfactory (*duḥkha*). Surely, a serious religious motivation underlay Nagarjuna's application of his dialectic to all philosophical views (*dṛṣṭi*).

Therefore, Nagarjuna did not intend his notion of Emptiness to be taken as a blanket injunction against the use of language. Even he talked about Emptiness. His point was that we should not create, and thereby cling to, linguistic permanencies in an impermanent universe of processive becoming. In other words, concepts, notions, doctrines, concepts, symbols, are necessary and may open the way to enlightenment—*if* we do not falsify reality into islands of permanency by clinging to concepts, notions, doctrines, concepts, and symbols.

The validity of my assertions is, of course, dependent upon what
Nagarjuna meant when he taught that an event, say a moment of human
experience, is empty. I think he meant several things which, incidentally,
are still operational notions in the Mahayana Buddhist world view. First,
the event is empty of "substance." That is, the separate moments of our
experience are not unified by an enduring self or "I" remaining self-iden-
tical through time, to which the experience "happens" or "belongs." A
moment of human experience represents only an event or a happening at
a particular moment of space-time.

Secondly, this means the experience lacks all possession, for whatever constitutes it does not belong to it. The particular elements of the
experience, its *dharmas,* are a coming together of what is other than the
experience.

Thirdly, the experience lacks all possessiveness. It imposes no form
on its constituting elements. Thus, it is empty of form because the form
of an experience results from what constitutes it.

Finally, the constituting elements of an experience are not the
"being" of that experience. Instead, the constituting elements *become* the
new experience, or better, this becoming *is* the experience. This also
means that the constituting elements of an experience do not have being
either, for they, too, are empty. Hence, Nagarjuna concluded that because there is no being, there are "no-things" to hang our words on,
nothing to capture verbally, but which we may nevertheless verbally
point to—*if* we do not cling to our linguistic-symbolic pointers. For
language, like everything else, is empty.

The point is not that there exists an implied world view in Nagarjuna's conception of the emptiness of all views. Indeed, it might be true
that von Brück's monistic interpretation of Nagarjuna's concept of Emptiness is a coherent interpretation of implied tendencies implicit in Mad-
hayamika thought which he only now makes explicit in the present essay.
But Nagarjuna was too consistent in applying his dialectic to his own
view of Emptiness to allow for this possibility. The result, therefore,
seems to be that von Brück's understanding of Emptiness as a source for
the paradigm shift he sees emerging in contemporary Buddhist thought is
based on a reading of Nagarjuna's teachings and subsequent Madhyamika tradition that neither Nagarjuna's teachings nor Madhyamika tradition can support. Accordingly, von Brück runs the risk of inventing a
Buddhist paradigm shift which Buddhist tradition cannot recognize.

Von Brück is, however, not alone in reading a monistic ontology
into Nagarjuna's thought. Most modern interpretations of Madhyamika

tradition, both Buddhist and non-Buddhist, are based on uncritically assumed monistice ontologies. The list is long and distinguished: D.T. Suzuki, Abe Masao, Hisamatsu Shin'ichi, Nishitani Keiji, Nishida Kitaro—all have read Madhyamika tradition through the eyes of either Hegel or Kant or both. Most Western interpreters have followed the lead of these important Buddhist teachers. But in my opinion, this is a distorted reading of Madhyamika thought. It may be, as I said above, that Nagarjuna's concept of Emptiness implies some sort of monistic ontology similar to the interpretations of Suzuki, Abe, Hisamatsu, Nishitani, and Nishida. But Nagarjuna would have said that their "views," too, are "empty." Asserting Nagarjuna's support for a monistic interpretation of Emptiness is a falsification of Buddhist tradition.

One can raise similar objections to von Brück's treatment of the Christian doctrine of the Trinity and the way he compares this doctrine to the "trinity" of the Buddhist *trikāya* doctrine. My question is, is von Brück reading the ontology of the Buddhist *trikāya* doctrine into mainline Christian trinitarian theology? It appears to me that he is, and in the process he fails to represent accurately the Christian doctrine of the Trinity and the Buddhist *trikāya* teaching. In so doing, he further undercuts dialogue between Buddhists and Christians.

Even in the writings of the Christian mystics of the Eastern Church, the Christian doctrine of the Trinity is not a metaphysical assertion about the nature of ultimate reality. It most certainly does not assume the monistic ontology that forms the foundation of von Brück's understanding of Christian trinitarian speculation. Specifically, the doctrine of the Trinity, at least according to mainline Christian versions, is a summary of the three interrelated ways of "being God" that God employs in God's relation to the world. God the Father symbolizes God as God is, God's "suchness," as it were, in contrast to the nature of all creatures in God's creation. God the Father is that which makes God God, or to use the language of Paul Tillich, God as the "ground of Being" whose nature is not reducible to any specific "being." God the Son symbolizes God's creative self-expression through Jesus as the Christ, the "Word" of God. God the Holy Spirit symbolizes God's continuing creative activity in the world, or God ceaselessly "doing" what God does in the present, or will do in the future.

There is nothing monistic about traditional Christian trinitarian tradition, even in Christian mysticism. In fact, if anything, the doctrine of the Trinity assumes a *dualistic* ontology, because it asserts a permanent, ontological distinction between God as creator, and everything else in the created order as creature. Forcing monistic assumptions upon the Christian doctrine of the Trinity distorts the historical role this doctrine has played in Christian experience.

Perhaps the source of the difficulties I perceive in von Brück's interpretation of the Christian doctrine of the Trinity lies in his comparison of this teaching with the Buddhist *trikāya* doctrine. The Mahayana Buddhist teaching of the "three bodies" may assume a monistic world view. The historical Buddhas (*nirmāṇakāya*) are concrete, space-time manifestations of more transcendent "bliss bodies" (*saṃbhogakāya*), or Buddhas dwelling in their respective "Buddha Lands." All Buddhas, historical Buddhas and Buddhas enjoying blissful existence in their Buddha Lands, are different forms of one *Dharmakāya,* or "Dharma body," the one reality unifying the existence of all Buddhas in their differences. Now while it may be true that such a monistic assumption is at the heart of Buddhist "trinitarian" Buddhology,[1] reading Christian trinitarian theology through the Buddhist *trikāya* doctrine falsifies both Christian and Buddhist self-understanding. It may be that Christian thought *ought* to be understood monistically, and that a monistic paradigm shift is occurring in Christian theology because of dialogue with Buddhist tradition. But *asserting* that the tradition itself supports such a monistic shift requires more careful and coherent demonstration than this essay provides.

In conclusion, von Brück has written an interesting, even provocative essay. I think he is absolutely correct. New paradigms are indeed being engendered in the Buddhist and Christian Ways because of their mutual dialogical encounter, as well as because of each religious Way's encounter with modern scientific theory. But I do not think von Brück's description of the nature of this paradigm is clear. I also do not think the arguments he employs to specify the nature of this new paradigm are coherent.

Note

1. *Editor's note:* This conclusion follows from Ingram's assumption that *Dharmakāya* is a single "reality," i.e., a *Grund* somewhat like the Hindu *Brahman.* But, *Dharmakāya* is often taught as a simile of *shūnyatā.* When this is the case, the philosophical basis of the *trikāya* doctrine is non-duality rather than monism.

Can Emptiness Will?

Roger Gregory-Tashi Corless

*T*here was a custom amongst my ancestors of relieving the long winter nights by singing of the deeds of old and making present those deeds in the singing. When the diners at a feast in the great grey wooden hall were full and content, the bards would sing to the glee-wood, and as the story unfolded and embellished itself, the glee-wood was passed to the thanes and the knights, from hand to hand they would pass it, and each man would sing according to his ability, bringing forth the past and so enlivening it. Thus the tree of their heritage grew and flowered, and a great shame it was to the man who could not sing.

There is a power in such songs, or myths, that mere facts cannot equal, so I wish to begin my essay with a song, and then to try to convert it into a philosophy. The song, I believe, will be true, but I do not know if I will be able to understand it, that is, I do not know if I can successfully shape it into a philosophy. If I cannot, dear reader, please return to my song, listen to it once more, and see if you can explain it better than I.

Then unto Hrothgar was the glee-wood passed,
And he sang both sooth and sad.

I sing sooth in that I sing of my own journey, and it is perhaps the journey of many. I sing sad with the sadness of my northern home that sighs to the tide and the sea-mews' calling, yet looks to the soft mist making earth and heaven one, and though it laments for death it wails with the wind and transfigures the sorrow in the grandness of its weeping.

My journey begins somewhere in ancient Britain. I proceed up, as some of the red-faced people of the New World do, through four worlds. The worlds are religions, and the worlds are consciousnesses. Finally I am in the clear darkness of space, where all riddles answer themselves in delicious laughter.

There I find the germ of the new vision. But I must plant it somewhere, and allow it to grow into a philosophy, so I journey with my question to the Buddhas and the Trinity, to find out if anything ever was. If they are gracious to me, I may be enabled to show you how to ask for yourself, "Can Emptiness Will?"

This is the dream of Hrothgar, child of Thor,
that he dreamed one winter, on the night
of Our Lady's snow-white conceiving:
and awoke, to tell of it.

The Dream

The First World was red, it was red through and throughout. No one knew whence it had come, but there were many stories about it. "It is red like the dawn, so it came from the sun." "It is red like blood, so it came from a Woman." "It is red like the earth, so it came out of the ground." But in any case, it was agreed that it was alive, that it would nurture if it were nurtured, and the people called it She. She had certain laws, and they were intractable. Or at least, they mostly were. Sometimes She could be persuaded to change Her mind, to give more or less rain, or sunshine, than She had intended. The priests knew how to humor Her, to petition Her, and to thank Her. And all the people were priests, that is to say, they all had a part to play in the dialogue with Her that rose and fell, went this way and that way, but never really ceased. Some of the people, however, were closer to Her than others, and on special days they would change their form and become more than human. On those days it was dangerous to go near them.

The humoring, the petitioning and the thanking was called Praise, and it was mostly song. Song in those days had power to create, it was not as it is now. Today our songs can change our minds and our hearts, but they are too weak to change our flesh. In those days, when the special people began to sing, and the rest of the people took up their song, the air became thicker, it became filled with liquid light that was first of all like a mist (a bright mist, not a cloudy mist) and then like a wind you could feel and grasp, and then it would gather itself together and become glowing pillars. As the song died away, the people found that they had built a stone temple out of the circle of their praise, and ever after the stones sang with them and for them. Even today this singing can sometimes be heard as one enters within such a circle. People now say they were observatories, since they point to the light. But they only point to the light because they came from the light. The stones are the children of the light. And, of course, they are round, like a woman, and they are stone, because they are earth. They are what the world was to the first people.

She wove her web and she gave and took. They called her Lady Wyrd. What she decreed seemed inescapable, or rather, what was inescapable was said to be the weaving of Wyrd. If something happened that could not have been foreseen by mortal eyes, a person would say "Wyrd wove me that." Because of this, the people could not grow. They were connected to everything in the web of Wyrd, but they could not escape from the web. They were slaves to themselves, though they did not know it.

Then one day a man called Hrothgar, the Warrior, met the Lady Wyrd and fell in love with her. He sang of her like this:

I met a lady in the meads,
  Full beautiful—a faery's child,
Her hair was long, her foot was light,
  And her eyes were wild.

He went with her to a hill which had a door, and through the door they both went, and there he slept.

She took me to her elfin grot,
  And there she wept, and sigh'd full sore,
And there I shut her wild wild eyes
  With kisses four.

He dreamed of death and battle, destruction and torment, and awoke forlorn, and wandered as if mad.

And this is why I sojourn here,
  Alone and palely loitering,
Though the sedge is withered from the lake
  And no birds sing.[1]

* * * * *

The Second World was white, it was white through and throughout. It was a world of ice and snow, calm and clear. Hrothgar wandered upon it, seeing no-one, until he met a sagely man dressed in a black cowl and carrying a shepherd's crook.

"Who are you, where am I, and why am I here?" asked Hrothgar of the old man.

"I am Benedict, he who has been blessed by the One God. You are here because you have subdued your passions by lulling the Lady Wyrd to sleep and have thus escaped from the World of Fire. But they will rise to trouble you again."

"Where are my people, the people of the First World?"

"They are within you; you and they have more to learn. Take now the name Gregory, the watchful." And the old man sang and said:

> I adore not the voice of birds,
> Nor sneezing, nor lots in this world,
> Nor a boy, nor lots, nor women:
>   My Druid is Christ, the Son of God,
>   Christ, Son of Mary, the Great Abbot,
>   The Father, the Son and the Holy Ghost.[2]

And he continued:

"Look into my face and see the vision which I will show you."

And Gregory looked and saw two roads. One led up toward the sun, and the other led down beneath the earth, back from where he had come. At the end of the road that led upward were beings all of light, beings who had not solidified their light, and all they did was to sing and to listen and sing again, and their song was in praise of a marvelous Lord who sat on a great throne below a great arch, and the Lord had a great blazing face burning like the sun and no body at all was there beneath it. That throne was set in a foursquare city, the walls of which were twelve thousand furlongs in length, in breadth and in height, foursquare it was like a crystal, and it shone with all the precious stones of which it was made (Rev 21:16–21). And the people in it were a kind and gentle people, and none had his back or his side to another, but all were face to face in perfect friendship and love. And they sang the songs which the Lord had given them, eight times in the day they sang them, at the proper hours.

The end of the road that led downward came to a deep and wide ravine full of fire with a bridge across it. Those who were charitable found it broad and easy, and they crossed over it and came round by a troublesome route to the city that was above. But those who were full of hate found the bridge as narrow as a razor's edge and they fell into the valley where they were tormented by beasts and demons and flames of their own imagining, yet were as real to them as themselves, and their cries were pitiful and prolonged.[3]

Then the vision ceased and Benedict said, "See how the first people enslaved themselves by worshiping the Lady Wyrd. You must now learn how the pain of this white world is the door to a third."

Then Gregory was led to a grassy mound on which the snow had fallen but lightly, and on it was a great Abbey. Inside the Abbey were the bones of a king and queen, and over their tomb was a cross. On the cross hung a dying and despised man, as it were a criminal, and blood flowed continually from the man's incurable wounds and filled the whole church with his pain and his suffering. He spoke to Gregory in the language of Hrothgar, "*Feala ic on tham beorge gebiden hæbbe wrathra wyrda*"[4] ("Many a terrible wyrd have I endured upon the hill") and then looked kindly on him and welcomed him.

Wyth a good chere oure good lorde lokyd in to hys syde and behelde with joy, and with hys swete lokying he led forth the vnderstandyng of hys creature by the same wound in to hys syd with in; and ther he shewyd a feyer and delectable place, and large jnow for alle mankynde that shalle be savyd and rest in pees and in loue.

And with this oure good lorde seyde well blessydfully: Lo how I loue the; as yf he had seyde, my darlyng, behold and see they lorde, thy god, that is thy maker and thy endlesse joy; see thyn owne brother, thy sauyoure; my chylde, behold and see what lykyng and blysse I hauve in thy saluacion, and for my loue enioye with me (Julian, 1978: 394–6).

So Gregory entered the side of the man and found himself in the same city which he had seen before. A glorious lady was therein, clothed with the sun, the moon of Wyrd beneath her feet, and on her head a crown of stars (cf. Rev 12:1). "I am the distillation of these snows," she said. "Sleep now, and I will lead you to the Third World."

*   *   *   *   *

The Third World was blue, it was blue through and throughout. In it there was nowhere to stand, for all the blue was water. Gregory floated upon the water, moving this way and that, until he saw rising from the waters a great tree bearing upon it as its fruits the objects of all his desires. On top of the tree was a large white lotus flower and on top of the lotus there were four white lions, each facing outward in a different direction. The lions bore on their backs a throne, and on the throne, with the moon as a cushion, sat a snow-white maiden sweetly smiling. She was richly clothed with queenly ornaments and had eyes in the palms of her hands, the soles of her feet, and the middle of her brow, as well as eyes in her face like a human's eyes. She sat cross-legged in the lotus pose and held her right arm downward with her palm open, and her left hand upraised, holding the stem of a blue lotus flower. Her body was all of white light and weightless, and from her heart she emitted suddenly, all at once like a shower of sparks, tens of hundreds of thousands of deities just like herself, so that the sky was filled with them.

"Who are you, where am I, and why am I here?" asked Gregory.

"I am Tara, she who carries sentient beings across the ocean of suffering. You are here because you have confronted your suffering and subdued it, but your subduing was like the taming of water by freezing it. The fire from the First World, which you had contained, rose and melted the ice of the Second World, and you would have drowned in suffering had you not taken refuge in the side of the Man Who Transfigures Suffering. Because you took refuge in him, you now float upon the waters of suffering and do not sink. These waters are the tears of Avalokiteshvara, the Compassionate One Who Hears The World's Laments, and from them I am born. You have now a share in this compassion. You are to be called Tashi, the Fortunate."

Then Tashi learned that although there is a basis, there is nowhere to stand. As the waves and the ocean are both real, and the waves and the ocean are neither the same nor different, so Form and Emptiness are both true and neither the same nor different. So also with suffering and bliss. His First World had been secure, but he had been moved about at the whim of Wyrd. By lulling her to sleep he had gained control over her and won the leisure to realize suffering as suffering rather than as an occasional punishment of Wyrd that was followed by pleasure. Suffering was as pervasive as the snows of the frozen Second World in which the passions were starved and contained.

But he had found there a Love which could overpower the petty passions of lust, hate and confusion. It was a Love which proceeded from a Being who was boundless and had no need to protect himself, for there was no vital center in which he could be wounded. And yet that Being restricted himself and allowed himself to bleed copiously with a wound that could not be cured until all his detractors had come to heal him by their embrace. Through this wound Gregory-Tashi had come, and now found himself pushed by the tides of Great Compassion from island to island of suffering beings who had stranded themselves by their fear of drowning. He wondered what had happened to the man with the wound and whether he too had been drowned, and if the great blazing face of the Lord in the crystal city had been put out in the flood. He asked himself again and again, "That boundless Being whom I saw, does he exist or not?" The more he asked himself this question "Does Being exist?" the more he sank beneath the waves of Great Compassion and experienced them as suffering. So he thought, "Compassion does not exist; Being is an illusion." But still somewhere in the depths of his misery a voice kept asking "Does That Being exist which is Being Itself?" until one day he gave up asking and sank like a stone to the very bottom of the ocean of suffering. Then the answer came: "The mind of That One is Emptiness. Therefore, how could it have anything to do with existence or non-existence?"

And the Third World vanished.

*   *   *   *   *

The Fourth World was clear, it was empty through and throughout. In it there were no things, and yet nothing was absent. Gregory-Tashi sang the song of his own death, for he was nowhere to be found:

On a green and kingly Tor there flowers a thorn:
On a cedared Master's mountain shines a vajra.
From one to the next is thirty years, as a human measures:
But when Mañjushri and Michael draw their swords,
They cannot find a hairsbreadth in between them.

Then Hrothgar awoke. It was the ninth of December, the morning after the Feast of Our Lady's Conception, and of the Day of Enlightenment, and there was snow.

*   *   *   *   *

I have just recounted a dream. In a dream, there are things, and there are things going on, but when we wake our common sense says, "Those were not things, and they did not go on." Chuang Tzu suspected that our whole life might be a dream (*Chuang Tzu* 2:11). Explanations of the universe, philosophy and theology, might be dreams of dreams. What sort of sense, common or uncommon, do we need to ask "Do the Buddhas, and God, *exist,* and do they *do* anything?" We cannot naively assume that they do, and we cannot do any comparisons until we have answered this question.

The Vision of the Stupa

Lotus Sutra 11, "The Appearance of a Stupa," presents us with precisely this problem. An enormous, baroquely ornate stupa, half as wide as it is tall, appears to the assembly of humans and non-humans, and a voice is heard coming from within it. Since a stupa is supposed to be a tumulus erected over a relic, the question naturally arises as to who or what is inside, authenticating the teaching of the Lotus Sutra by the Buddha Shakyamuni. After a space during which emanation—or replica —Shakyamunis manifest elsewhere and travel to the site in question in order to make offerings, just as they would during a standard visualisation-liturgy, the "real" Shakyamuni opens up the stupa and reveals the supposedly extinct Buddha Prabhutaratna sitting inside, quite healthy and talkative although he had passed into perfect nirvana incalculable aeons ago ("they saw a Buddha who had nirvanated more than 10^7 crores of immeasurable kalpas ago," T.9:33c3) and who had come just for the purpose of hearing this Sutra taught. The purport of the Sutra, as Prabhutaratna had said while still immured in the stupa, is the bodhisattva-dharma which the Buddhas have mindfully protected and which they teach with great *samatā* wisdom (T.9:32b28–9). Shakyamuni then asks if anyone can spread this teaching throughout the human realm "right now, this very minute" (the Chinese is very insistent) for he is shortly to go into nirvana himself. In the following verses (which are probably an earlier stratum of the text) this question is asked by *all* the Buddhas of *everyone* in the Great Assembly, and each individual is asked to make a vow in this regard (T.9:33c13–14; 34a4–6).

The issues raised here are profound. If there is no nirvana, no hope would be known for those trapped in samsara (*Udāna* 80:3). If, on the other hand, nirvana exists and is liberation, it is beyond the duality of suffering and not-suffering, of this and that, and if it is beyond this and that, a nirvanated person cannot speak of it, and therefore, once again, no hope would be known for those trapped in samsara. But, Prabhutaratna has nirvanated, yet he speaks. Shakyamuni is about to nirvanate, and is afraid he will not be able to speak from out of that beyond. So, the question is, how is Dharma spoken of? Who will vow to teach it, indeed who *can* teach it? Can it be taught? Logically, it cannot; yet we do in fact hear it. The Mahayana sutras pose this problem of the *procession by non-procession* of Dharma into samsara, but do not explicate it.

Nagarjuna is of assistance here. He takes an apparently much simpler problem: does *anything* "go"? Commonsensically, many things appear to go. But, he asks us, where is the going by which something goes? That is, where is the force that moves things? It could be in the past, the present or the future. But to say it is in the future is absurd, for the goer has by then already gone. So it may be in the past. But then the going would have ceased before the thing which goes has begun going, and the going could not make the goer go. Therefore, it must be in the present. If it is in the present, it must be either the same as the thing going or different from it. But if it is the same as the thing going it *is* the thing going, it is just a synonym for it. If it is different from the thing going, first of all it has no contact with the thing going, and so it cannot make the thing go (unless the goer and the going are linked by an intermediary which is made to go by the going and makes the goer go, but then there would have to be an infinite number of such intermediaries, and the goer would never go because the going would never reach it) and secondly there could be going without a goer, which is absurd. Thus, "going" *cannot be found* and must be recognized as empty (cf. *Mūlamadhyama-kakārikāḥ* 2 with Candrakirti's commentary).

Note that Nagarjuna does not say that nothing goes, for then his argument would not go either. Prasangika Madhyamika is smarter than that. It waits for the metaphysician laboriously to assemble his metaphysic, then it gleefully gives it a push and it all falls down. B.K. Matilal has called this "rejection" rather than denial. It is a *prasajya-pratishedha,* which Jeffrey Hopkins translates as "non-affirming negative." Technically, "going" is neither present nor absent nor both nor neither, it is *empty,* that is, it is space-like. It occurs, but it does not occur because of anything.

Things also, according to this teaching, are space-like, and so is the Dharma. The Lotus Sutra is objecting to the reification of the Dharma by opponents it calls Hinayanists, who, among other cosy viewpoints, neatly box up samsara and nirvana as different *things.* At the level of elementary teaching, such as the use of Jataka to teach basic morality, this is a useful *upāya,* but as we purify our consciousness we see problems with it—specifically, how can non-duality be or not be preached without becoming falsified as duality, or monism, or any of the other mistakes negated in the eightfold negation of the *vandana* which opens the *Mūlamadhyama-kakārikāḥ?* The answer of Mahayana is that all is empty, i.e., all is as it is, just as it is, and the movement which we see is the movement of our mind. This is a *real movement* but it is *not essentially reifiable.* As in the koan about the flag: does the wind move it, or does it move the wind? Neither, our minds are moving. Yet, the flag still flaps in the breeze (*Mumonkan,* case 29).

That is why Prabhutaratna says that the Lotus Sutra teaches Bodhisattva-style Buddhism, i.e., the Mahayana, which is guarded in the *minds* of the Buddhas, and which is taught with extremely sharp and piercing teaching which is *samatā,* i.e., fundamentally event-less.

This begins to answer the question of whether Hrothgar's dream was real or not, i.e., whether myth is real or not, or whether reality is or is not. But let us hold this in reserve for a while and ask the Christians whether God is or is not, whether he does anything, and whether anyone preaches the Gospel.

The Vision in the Hekhal

The Biblical God is not primarily, or even mainly, a God who is, but a God who does. Whoever it was who first translated Exodus 3:14 as "I AM WHO I AM" (as the R.S.V. still does, capital letters and all), that is,

"I am He Who Exists From Himself, the Uncaused Cause," committed a linguistic howler of such enormity that it deserves to go in the *Guinness Book of Records* as the World's Most Misleading Mistranslation. Because of it, generations of Christians have found it impossible to distinguish the warm and caring God of the Bible from the cold, abstract God of Greek philosophy and have further tormented themselves over whether God's existence is a predicate of him, or of anything, or not. But the Hebrew is in the incomplete or continuous mode (the so-called imperfect tense) and means rather "I am He Who will always be present." Presence, doing and action are of the being of the Biblical God. Thus, this God sends forth, and he looks for people to be sent forth.

The *locus classicus* of sending forth is the call of First Isaiah, recorded in Isaiah 6. In 740 B.C.E., as the great King Uzziah of Judah was dying, Isaiah was attending a grand liturgy for YHWH in the *Hekhal* (temple, literally "palace"), when the physical scene changed for him and he saw God on a high throne, attended by semi-anthropoid winged creatures called seraphim. These creatures "cried each to each and said 'Holy! Holy! Holy! YHWH of Heavenly Armies! Full is all the earth with his glory!' " (Is 6:3, my translation). Isaiah felt the ground shake and the place filled with incense smoke. He was dismayed, for to see such power nakedly is to be destroyed by it, but a seraph flew to him and purified his *mouth* (*peh,* not his eyes or heart) so as to protect and prepare him for his mission. God then asked "Whom shall I send out, and who will go for us?" (Is 6:8). Isaiah, of course, goes. But, we have to ask, does he really?

In order to answer this question, we will allow ourselves to descend beneath the surface meaning (*sensus literalis*) to the spiritual meaning (*sensus plenior*) (what Buddhists would call moving from *nitārtha* to *neyārtha*), a procedure which is of great antiquity and which I have argued cannot be given up without peril to our entire understanding of what a sacred text is all about (Corless, 1979).

Isaiah is commanded, after he has expressed his willingness in verse 8, to proclaim the *fact* that God's glory, his *kabod* or shining brilliance which is a kind of divine plasma surrounding him wherever he goes, is *already* filling the earth. Isaiah has seen this, and he is to make others see it, but he is warned that they will not, even should he proclaim it until civilization dies out (vv. 9–12). In an ironic figure, he is told to make the people blind and deaf by his message—i.e., their resistance will be such that they will refuse the love and the joy he is to take to them. (A Buddhist might comment, "Of course: beginningless ignorance is indeed perverse like that.") Isaiah's preaching comes after his mouth has been purified by a hot stone from the burning altar. His mouth, or speaking, would then have taken on the nature of the divine fire which touched it. Parts of this vision have been incorporated into the Christian Eucharist. God is visualized as enthroned and surrounded by seraphim, and clouds of incense are offered to him. The people sing the song of the seraphim (the *Sanctus*) and, in the Greek Liturgy of Saint John Chrysostom, the priest tells himself, after he has received the living fire of the Body and Blood of God, "This has touched my lips, and my lawlessness *shall be* removed and my sin *shall be* purified." Thus the Christian *sensus plenior* interpretation of the Biblical passage (using the principle of *lex orandi, lex credendi*) is that it describes the action of the Trinity (thus the thrice repeated "Holy") as God *makes pure* what already *is pure*. I have previously proposed that both the Christian and the Buddhist spiritual life can be viewed as a *progress toward* what *already is,* and that this procession-without-procession can be understood on the model of the divine co-inherence of the Persons of the Trinity (*perichōrēsis*), and of the empty coterminality of samsara and nirvana according to *Mūlamadhyamakakārikāḥ* 25:20 (Corless, 1985). What I am concerned with here is whether or not *God* moves at all when he "acts" by contacting his creation.

Nicholas of Cusa asked somewhat the same question and left us his reflections in his *De Visione Dei,* "On the Vision of God, or The Icon." An icon is a representation of a Christian vision which participates in that vision. It is, if you will, a painted sacrament which effects what it signifies, very much as is a Tibetan *thang-kha*—indeed, the treatment of space, the technique, and the ascesis preliminary to painting are remarkably similar for both icon and *thang-kha.* "The icon is an image of a mysterious, heavenly vision, a hymn of praise, a manifestation," says Saint John of Damascus. "The icon is both the way and the means; it is prayer itself," says a modern interpreter (Ouspensky and Lossky, 1952: 40). Thus, in contemplating an icon as an aid to contemplating God, Nicholas was living at the heart of the Christian vision.

Nicholas observes that the eyes of an icon always seem to be upon us. No matter how we move, they do not leave us, yet they do not themselves move. If two people look at the same icon, each reports that he alone is being regarded. If these people move about the room, the eyes will seem to follow each simultaneously, even if they move contrary to each other. Thus, says Nicholas, does God see us all individually while seeing us all collectively. This leads him to contemplate how God in eternity relates to creatures in time, in chapter 11, entitled "How God Is Seen in Succession without Succession." A clock, he says, contains all time as a concept yet strikes particular hours in a definite and predictable sequence. So "that which is succession in the clock existeth without succession in the word or concept (of 'clock')." Sequential time is "enfolded" in the concept "clock" and "unfolded" in the action of the clock. This is like Eternity. "Eternity, therefore, both enfoldeth and unfoldeth succession, since the concept of the clock, which is eternity, doth alike enfold and unfold all things." And so for the Christian mission, and the going of God:

> ... I return again to find Thee beyond the wall of the coinci-
> dence of enfolding and unfolding, and as I go in and go out by
> this door of Thy word and Thy concept, I find sweetest nour-
> ishment. When I find Thee as the power that unfoldeth, I go
> out: when I find Thee as the power that alike enfoldeth and
> unfoldeth, I go in and go out alike. I go in, passing from the
> creatures to Thee, their Creator, from effects to the Cause; I go
> out, passing from Thee, the Creator, to the creature, from Cause
> to effects. I go in and go out simultaneously when I perceive
> how going out is one with going in, and going in with going out.
> I see Thou dost neither enfold nor unfold, whether separately or
> together. For distinction and conjunction alike are that wall of
> coincidence, *beyond which* Thou existest, set free from all that
> can be spoken or thought (Dolan, 1962: 152, my emphasis).

This is still a little confused, however, for Nicholas distinguishes Cause and effect, and identifies Cause with God and effect with creatures, while throwing in something about "beyond all that," as if he wonders if he hasn't got it right. Nagarjuna, in his *Twelve Gate Treatise* chapter 10, assures Nicholas that his position is unintelligible.

> If God is self-existent, He should need nothing. If He needs
> something, He should not be called self-existent. If He does not
> need anything, why did He (cause) change, like a small boy who
> plays a game, to make all creatures? ... Thus, there are various
> causal conditions which make things. You should know that all
> things are not made by God and also that God does not exist
> (Cheng, 1982: 97, 99).

Nicholas has become trapped in his Platonism. We should go back to the vision. Mother Julian spoke out of this vision when she said:

> And thus oure good lorde answeryd to alle the questyons and dow3tys that I myght make, sayeng full comfortabely; I may make alle thyng wele, and I can make alle thyng wele, and I shall make alle thyng wele, and I wylle make alle thyng welle; and thou shalt se thy selfe that alle maner of thyng shalle be wele. There he seyth: I may, I vnderstonde for the father; and there he seyth: I can, I vnderstond for the sonne; and there he seyth: I wylle, I vnderstonde for the holy gost; and there he seyth: I shalle, I vnderstonde for the vnyte of the blessyd trinite, thre persons and oon truth; and there he seyth: Thou shalt se thy selfe, I vnderstond the (onyng) of alle man kynde that shall be sauyd in to the blyssedfulle trynite (Julian, 1978: 417).

What she means, as Brant Pelphrey perceptively explains, is that the Christian becomes himself wrapped in the self-en-wrapping (*perichōrēsis*) of the Holy Trinity. This movement of the Trinity within Himself is not, as Aquinas clearly says, a real movement at all:

> The term *procession* within the Blessed Trinity signifies a coming forth from a principle and not necessarily a going out to an object, though the coming forth of the Holy Spirit, a coming forth of love, does imply a going forth to another, namely to the beloved (Gilby, 1958: sec. 125).

That is, as Julian has it, there are two "comings" (or "goings") in God: one is intradeical, the procession of the Trinity in and around Himself; another is extradeical, a procession in and around creatures in love. She calls these "two secrets," and says that the second is revealed in Jesus while the first "is hyd and sparryd from vs" (Julian, 1978: 415) since it has not to do with our salvation. Technically, the intradeical secret is the intrinsically unknowable apophatic perichoresis and the extradeical secret is the cataphatic perichoresis. Julian's vision is that participation in the cataphatic perichoresis takes us up into the apophatic perichoresis so that, as experienced by creatures, "it is a process, but in the unknowable Trinity it is something which has already taken place, in the person of the Son of God" (Pelphrey, 1982: 125).

What appears to have been seen by Julian is that the apophatic and cataphatic *perichōreses* (if that is how we may form the Anglo-Greek plural) are themselves in a relation of perichoresis, such that there is a procession-without-procession. This corrects Nicholas' fatal slip about a *Causa Sui* by showing that the connection between divine Cause and creaturely effect is empty. Thus we can assert the following principle:

> *The perichōrēsis of the apophatic and cataphatic perichōrēsis of the Triune God allows the Triune God to self-exist and to cause things while escaping Nagarjuna's destruction of Ishvara.*

The vision of Isaiah has then the same ontological status as the appearance of Prabhutaratna, and the Triune God goes in and out in Emptiness as the Buddha (*Tathāgata*) is both Thus Gone (*Tathā-gata*) and Thus Come (*Tathā-āgata*). Since the fundamental going-in-and-coming-out of God for the Christian is Christ, and since Christ, as the Logos, is the manner in which the Triune God knows himself from all eternity in his perichoresis, the incarnation of Christ is the enfleshment of this intradeical self-knowing. Since this self-knowing is empty in its perichoresis, we can understand *John* 6:14, "The Logos became flesh," as "*In Christ, Emptiness became flesh,*" which has as its corollary, "*The Mind of Christ is Emptiness.*"

This *emphatically does not mean* that Emptiness is God, or indeed that Emptiness and God have anything whatever to do with each other, since Emptiness is not a thing and God is not a thing, so that any comparison of them as the same or different or both or neither is illicit from the outset. It does mean, however, that what Buddhists experience epistemologically as Emptiness is experienced ontologically by Christians as Christ, and that to understand the Mind of Christ we need to understand Emptiness, and in order to understand Emptiness we need to understand the actions of Christ. If this seems a little strange, I suggest you work with the following koan, which came to me during Mass on the Third Sunday of Easter, 1982:

> If God saw himself before Eternity, how many eyes would he see?

What I appear to be saying (and I am trying to explicate something, so I am not sure I have it right) is that the Mind of Christ and Emptiness, that is to say the Gospel and the Dharma, are complementary to each other, not as yin and yang which replace or imply each other, but perichoretically, or co-inherently, such that each is autonomous and without need of the other, but each can somehow illuminate the other so as to establish the other on a surer foundation. This seems to be what I was aiming at when I proposed that Buddhism and Christianity fulfilled each other in co-inherent superconsciousness (Corless, 1986).

What kind of paradigm do we then have? For that, it will be helpful to examine what physicists are now proposing about the nature of the universe.

Can Emptiness Will?

Our presently observed reality (known directly or through instruments) is, for the physicist David Bohm, an explicate order which is "a comparatively small pattern of excitation" read out of an implicate order which is multi-dimensional and perhaps infinite. Explicate order is itself multiple and can arrange itself as "relatively autonomous sub-totalities" any one of which "may up to a point be studied in its own right" (Bohm, 1980: 192–3). The implicate order contains the possibilities for any number of explicate orders, yet each explicate order is a creative projection "which unfolds into a sequence of moments that is not completely derivable from what came earlier in this sequence or set of such sequences" (Bohm, 1980: 212). This implicate order is "the ground of all that is" (Bohm, 1980: 212). Explicate orders, once they are explicate, operate not randomly but according to three key features:

1. A set of implicate orders.
2. A special distinguished case of the above set, which constitutes an explicate order of manifestation.
3. A general relationship (or law) expressing a force of necessity which binds together a certain set of the elements of the implicate order in such a way that they contribute to a common explicate end (different from that to which another set of inter-penetrating and intermingling elements will contribute) (Bohm, 1980: 195).

The extent to which this paradigm works for physics is a problem for physicists. Its importance to us is the way in which it might illuminate the relationship of Buddhism and Christianity, specifically Emptiness and the Triune Deity's Perichoresis, as autonomous yet co-inherent. It needs to be stressed that Bohm proposes holonomy as a *paradigm* for physics.

This paradigm can itself be no more than a paradigm for (or *prajñapti* of) the Buddhist understanding of reality. I will examine the above three features of Bohm's paradigm in terms of its possible use as an illumination of a resonance between the Buddhist Emptiness and the Christian Trinity.

1. A Set of Implicate Orders

Bohm refers to the implicate order in ontological terms: it is "this higher-dimensional ground," "the immense multidimensional ground" and "the ground of all that is" (Bohm, 1980: 209, 211, 212). These terms are incompatible with Emptiness and, although they have a theistic ring to them, they are incompatible with Triune Deity's Perichoresis as we here understand it. But, this may simply be Bohm's failure to follow the full implications of his own model. Let us suppose as follows. Explicate order S is unfolded from an implicate order which functions for it as the metasystem S_1. This in turn is unfolded from an implicate order which functions as the metasystem S_2. This process can be imagined as continuing to S_n where "n" is large but finite. S_n would then be something like the Vedantic Brahman, or the Prakṛti of Samkhya before it vibrates under the influence of Purusha, or the Causa Sui posited by classical Western philosophy in order to end an inadmissible infinite regress. This is in effect Ken Wilber's understanding of the process, such that he can call the holomovement another form of the *philosophia perennis* (Wilber, 1982: 157–186). Such a statement, when given to Nagarjuna, disappears like an Amazonian bearer amongst the piranhas. However, we could set n = ∞, when there would be no end to the process, and we would not in fact have a holistic interpretation at all. Bohm seems to be occasionally on the point of doing this, but he does not come clean and say whether he wishes to do this or not. Thirdly, we could imagine a series of metasystems S, S_1, S_2 · · · · · S_n where n → ∞, i.e., where "n" becomes asymptotic as it tends to infinity. In this case, there could be a condition S_ϕ, i.e., a null set, outside of the domain U (i.e., all possible sets of S_n with n < ∞).

This third possibility would agree with Buddhism as follows. In all the accounts of the parinirvana of Shakyamuni Tathagata there is the curious report of how he ascends through the stages of meditation (*dhyāna*) but does not enter final nirvana (*parinirvāṇa*) until he descends them and ascends them again. *Parinirvāṇa* is evidently discontinuous with the set of the four *dhyānas* which culminates in *bhavāgra* ("the vanishing point of Being"). Similarly, the four formless attainments (*ārūpyasamāpatti*) are routinely described by Buddhism as conditions of high spiritual attainment yet still intra-samsaric. Complete liberation (*vimoksha*) is somehow outside them, even outside, or beyond, the unimaginably rarefied condition of the highest formless attainment, "the state of neither thinking nor not thinking" (*naivasaṃjñānāsaṃjñāyatana*). We might say that the Buddhist criticism of Hinduism, specifically of Hindu monism in the form practiced by the "heretical teachers" Arada Kalama and Udraka Ramaputra, is that it mistakes the asymptotic *bhavāgra* for the null set of *vimoksha*. And perhaps the Gradualists of Chinese Buddhism were focusing on the asymptotic segment of the path while the Subitists were emphasizing the quantum leap to the null set. As the koan puts it: "When the ten thousand things return to the One, to where does the One return?" The answer, I think, is { }. and certainly not {0}, which would be Nihilism.

Christianly, the apophatic perichōrēsis is such a null set which is intrinsically not open to investigation by any except God himself, and when God sees philosophers straining to look into this perichōrēsis, Mother Julian says simply that "oure lord hath pitte and compassion on vs for that some cretures make them so besy therin" (Julian, 1978: 415). The trick, of course, of living a fully God-directed life is not to give up on the asymptotic investigation of the cataphatic perichōrēsis with a *premature* "inshallah" while at the same time recognizing it as an asymptote. Or, as Dogen would put it, to practice zazen just because, in the perspective of the "Time-Being" (*uji*), I am already enlightened.

2. A Special Distinguished Case of the Above Set

Having established what the implicate order is for Buddhism and Christianity (whatever it might be for physics, or Hinduism, or any other explicate system) the rest of the model arranges itself. Both Buddhism and Christianity presuppose an implicate order which explicates as basically supportive or loving, as I believe I have shown (Corless, 1985). The explicate Christian order then unfolds to manifest a loving Triune God and the explicate Buddhist order unfolds to manifest the co-terminality in Emptiness of suffering and bliss. These two explicate orders are autonomous and incompatible.

3. A Common Explicate End

Any particular explicate subset, or relatively autonomous sub-totality, functions according to certain laws that necessarily bind its elements toward a common explicate end. The more a Christian practices Christianity, the more the loving activity of the Triune God becomes present, meaningful and actual to him, and the more a Buddhist practices Buddhism, the more the co-terminality of samsara and nirvana as shunyata becomes present, meaningful, and actual to him. Conversely, the more the presuppositions of all incompatible relatively autonomous sub-totalities become meaningless. If we regard these sub-totalities as partial truths, with the implicate order as the "true truth," or the sub-totalities as illusory misrepresentations of the implicate order which is the "true truth," we have denied the whole principle of Emptiness and the Apophatic Perichōrēsis and have escaped from the contemplation of the implicate order, back into a universe of materially imaginable things. It seems, however, that in the *theōsis* ("divinization" in Orthodoxy; "sanctification" in Catholicism) of the Christian practice and the *bodhi* (enlightenment) of the Buddhist practice a quantum leap into the null set is made at some point and, like the solving of a koan, the question "Can Emptiness Will?" becomes irrelevant by reason of the disappearance of the questioner.

Which Dreamed It?

"Your Red Majesty shouldn't purr so loud," Alice said, rubbing her eyes, and addressing the kitten, respectfully, yet with some severity. "You woke me out of oh! such a nice dream! And you've been along with me, Kitty—all through the Looking-Glass world. Did you know it, dear?" (Carroll, 1963: 341).

The problem which presents itself to Alice after returning from a world in which everything is backward yet somehow makes sense is: who was (or is) who? Which world is real? Within Alice's dream the Red King has a dream of Alice, and like Chuang Tzu and the butterfly, Alice cannot decide who dreamed who. This is the question with which I opened the more formal part of this essay, but, like Kitty, it has been with us all along.

Mechanism regards the world of sensory experience as objective and real, and states that our minds can have "clear and distinct ideas" which faithfully reflect objective reality. Idealism allows the reality of mental events only, and denies either that objective reality exists at all or, in a modified form called Representationalism, denies that we can have any clear and distinct idea of objective reality although it permits objective reality to exist. According to Mechanism, Chuang Tzu dreamt he was a butterfly, and the Red King was a part of Alice's dream. According to Idealism, Chuang Tzu was, or maybe still is, a butterfly, and Alice was dreamt by the Red King—who was perhaps dreamt by somebody else, and so on and so on. Either way, madness lies. Mechanism presents us with a dead universe—so Whitehead's disgust with a universe of "endlessly hurrying matter"—and if we ever actually see this, as I have now and again, we awake to the terror of being the only conscious entity in an infinity of robots. Idealism, on the other hand, lets anything be anything, and if I feel I am Louis XIV you cannot be so impertinent as to tell me I am not or I shall have your head.

Western philosophers have customarily tried to escape from these two impossible scenarios and finish the play by trundling God onto the stage, and the *dieu des philosophes et des savants* is a *deus ex machina* if ever there was one. George Berkeley protected the general predictability of ordinary experience by supposing that God observed everything and so he arranged it that balls thrown in the air would hit the ground even if no creature observed them.

But, as Pascal might say, Berkeley's observant *deus otiosus* has nothing whatever to do with the Being of Light (his form is not described) who invited Isaiah to go forth and proclaim his glory. Nor, indeed, does Descartes' God, although he has a much busier schedule, since it is his job to relate external matter and subjective consciousness by innumerable little acts of creation causing us to have all those clear and distinct ideas that we think we have. But since, as Bohm dryly remarks, this function of God has been abandoned by science "it has not commonly been noticed that thereby the possibility of comprehending the relationship between matter and consciousness has collapsed" (Bohm, 1980: 197). Bohm then proposes that both matter and consciousness are relatively autonomous sub-totalities unfolded out of the seamless implicate holomovement. This is useful to his purposes, and it is seminal to ours.

I have proposed that Buddhism and Christianity can be understood as relatively autonomous sub-totalities unfolded from an implicate order which manifests itself as loving and supportive. As autonomous, these sub-totalities have their own authenticity, have no need of each other, are not aspects of each other, and indeed (except in the moral realm) are incompatible with each other. Nevertheless, they have a formal (rather than actual) co-inherence, perichoresis or empty co-terminality, in the implicate holomovement. This co-inherence cannot be described or visualized, for it is neither an object nor a subject, but it can be a subjectless and objectless *experience* as a *satori*. As a satori is an experience, in fact, The Experience, but not an experience *of* anything *by* anybody, so we can "enter" through the Door of the Non-Binary Thing (*Vimalakīrtinirdesha* 8) into the null set of the holomovement as an experience, given the proper preparation. Christianly, we can say with Jan van Ruysbroeck that we can enter heaven only by leaving our intellects and emotions at its gates.

Summary

What I have tried to do in this essay is simultaneously to demonstrate the possibility of such an experience and create an environment in which it might occur. I began with a dream, unhitching you from familiar reality while allowing you to retain the feeling of having a lifeline back to it. The dream accessed our common planetary memory as beings whose consciousness has evolved from the rocks and is still evolving, so that we can, in a general way, recapitulate our common history in our individual mental universes just as if (as may in fact be the case) we have a common memory enfolded in our psycho-genetic make-up which we can unfold by being open to what we generally call our unconscious, and which we consciously contact in myth, symbol and dream.

Since I am British, it was natural for me here to base my unconscious on Celtic and Anglo-Saxon mythic structures. The fundamental vision of my ancestors, as I understand it, was that heaven is on earth, would we take time to see it. The extended dawn and dusk of latitude 53.5° N, where I was born in this life, is, as the Roman invaders discovered, conducive to meditation. The languorous mingling of light and dark have no discernible barrier. The winter fogs prolong the night into the day and somehow illuminate the night when it returns. There is then a sense of the co-inherence of death and life expressed in the bitter-sweet nature poetry of the Celts and which I have sensed elsewhere, with perhaps a sharper edge, in the Japanese emotion of *sabi*. My song arose from this joyful sadness which I still feel when I return home, despite the recent surgery of the motorways.

The feeling I then extended upward, like the opening of the *chakras*, through my experiences with Christianity and Buddhism. When I stand in the little church of the Holy Cross, Woodchurch, Wirral, which was built on a Druid mound and dedicated about 600 C.E. to the Celtic Saint Tecwyn, and which bowed stiffly but never fully, "with patient, deep disdain," to the coming of the Papists and their expulsion by the Reformers, I hear again the Druid wailing in the psaltery of Anglican Chant, and there is present to me a British Christianity which absorbed and transformed in acerbic grace the stern legalism and sugary devotions of the Mediterranean. I tried to communicate this herein by quoting Mother Julian in her original Middle English within the setting of Glastonbury Abbey, set on its ancient tor dedicated to the Celtic dragon and to Saint Michael his gentle rider, and containing the reputed bones of Arthur and Guinevere.

My Christianity at that level was immature and concerned itself with a negative ascesis and the duality between freedom and imprisonment, similar to the Hinayana phase of Mahayana practice. Thus I had to move up again and doubt God as I tried to look into Emptiness. This produced in me a crisis of deep depression and severe isolation, when suddenly, as Hakuin Zenji kept whispering to me, at the very bottom of my inability to answer the koan I had set myself—namely, "Who is Christian or Buddhist?"—I found that there was no bottom, and I had disappeared. Thus I sang the "Verse of Great Death" recounting my pilgrimage from Glastonbury Tor to Mount Koya, which was no pilgrimage at all. Throughout my journey there was a Kitty, but a more noble one than Alice's. Psychologists might wish to call her my anima in appropriate transformations, but I prefer to call her by her name as she successively appeared to me and aided me: the Lady Wyrd, Our Lady Saint Mary, and the Lady Tara. To them in gratitude this essay is dedicated.

Notes

1. The verses are from "La Belle Dame sans Merci" by John Keats.
2. The incantation is attributed to Saint Columba.
3. Gregory's vision is based upon *The Vision of Adamhnán Ó Tinne* (Jackson, 1971: selection 231).
4. From *The Dream of the Rood.*

Can Will Be Predicated of Emptiness? A Response to Roger Corless

Durwood Foster

Let me begin by gratefully saluting the deep participatory knowledge Professor Corless brings to bear on his theme, a knowledge embracing both technical competence and experiential insight. I also affirm the autobiographical mode of this essay. For the cross-cultural path we want to traverse in books like the present one, the sharing of our personal stories has great value. Then, too, Professor Corless' use of poetic imagination and dream material, along with a kind of playful conceptual spontaneity, is not beside the point. If a wider ecumenism of religions is to succeed, I believe something like a Jungian entelechy has to emerge from our unconscious—creating new syntheses of our ultimate symbols. In brooding and musing one's way toward such syntheses, Professor Corless is, moreover, absolutely right to invoke the new physics, as he does principally through the use of David Bohm. Not only would it be counterproductive to essay religious unity apart from our current science; the latter, as Corless discerns, is a potent catalyst of spiritual insight. And while Bohm's work in particular has not won universal assent among physicists, its heuristic impact is salutary both within and beyond its own core discipline.

Let me further commend the overall balance in Professor Corless' essay between his recognition of ineffable mystery (the apophatic super-consciousness, the peace that passes understanding, or the ultimate implicate order) and his espousal on the other hand of the meaningfulness of penultimate religious symbolization and conceptualization. There is a depth beyond God and Emptiness that transcends all possible description, but this neither annuls nor demeans the rational investigation of ultimacy, which proceeds asymptotically towards its transrational goal. Surely the dialectical affirmation of *both* mystery *and* specifiable meaning is essential to the theological enterprise.

It is, moreover, in good keeping with the spirit of the dialogue that Professor Corless proposes to bless mutually both Buddhism and Christianity without in any way reductively consolidating them. This stance, however successful its more particular thematization may turn out to be, exemplifies well the "paradigm shift" to a genuine pluralism that many experience today in interreligious relations. It is more and more frequently affirmed that ultimacy is actually encountered by one and the same person through ostensibly disparate symbol systems, so that numerous persons of theological sophistication attest themselves to be, for example, both Christian and Buddhist in some significant sense and degree. I personally believe this to be a wholesome trend and hope it will continue, as I expect it to.

It seems to me Professor Corless is also right to suggest that the Christian trinitarian notion of perichōrēsis is an apt conceptual model of the emerging new paradigm. According to this notion, the "persons" of the Trinity are full instantiations of the Divine essence, yet each is irreducibly distinct. Corless likewise proposes that Buddhist Emptiness (*shūnyatā*) is a parallel model, since in it non-duality and the phenomenal world are both affirmed inasmuch as their ultimate difference is annulled or transcended. As with the trinitarian persons, we might say their "essence" (that is, what the non-dual and the phenomenal really are) is the same. In an analogous way, Corless would affirm the real difference of Buddhism and Christianity, and yet also annul that difference ultimately—that is to say, by reference to their transcendental "essence." It goes without saying that in all such formulations terms like "essence" are problematic and may be immediately attacked by those who hold this or that fixed notion of what given terms mean. Certainly an enormous labor of conceptual analysis challenges us in trying to establish what the trinitarian "essence" means over against the three "hypostases" which somehow differentiate it, or what *shūnyatā* means in relation to nirvana and samsara, which ostensibly differentiate it. Nevertheless, in my judgment, Professor Corless' suggestion is heuristically penetrating and apt, and symbolizes well the fundamental intuition that motivates many in the mutual espousal of, or at least categorical respect for, *both* Buddhism and Christianity.

Turning now to some points of difficulty with the paper, I am troubled by the handling of causality, which is repugnant to Professor Corless as a way of conceiving God's relation to the world. I agree that causality is not an adequate and certainly not an exclusive way of construing this relation. Plausible to me is Tillich's proposal that being, that is, the ground or power of being, so understood as to transcend both causality *and* substance, offers a more adequate conceptual symbolism to express what Christians have called God's creation of the world. But Corless's adamant rejection of causality seems to be predicated on a reduction (*à la* the "mechanical paradigm" of Newtonian science which he otherwise rejects) of causality to *efficient* causality. Even in that one restricted mode, I believe there is a place for causality in envisaging God's relation to the world, though it certainly does not meet the entire need. But my main plea in this connection would be for a restoration of causality to the differential richness that Aristotle classically accorded it in recognizing formality, materiality and finality as also belonging to the generic notion, along with efficiency. It may be that Aristotle's fourfold schema needs supplementation or reconception today; possibly there are other species of cause, for example, the reciprocity of part and whole. In any case, there is no reason to think that cause, whether or not more richly conceived, should be the only way of expressing the God-world relation. I am merely suggesting that it not be altogether dropped from theology's conceptual-symbolic repertory; and I see no reason to pillory it, except where it was misused both in reductionistic and exclusivistic ways. As St. Thomas says, *abusus non tollit usus.*

To move to another point, Professor Corless maintains that "Berkeley's observant *deus otiosus* has nothing whatever to do with the Being of light . . . who invited Isaiah to go forth to proclaim his glory." I disagree, and I think this is another point where Professor Corless is at cross purposes with himself. Berkeley's God is not otiose, in my opinion, certainly no more so than the non-causal God or Emptiness that Corless desiderates, but is in fact an interesting conceptual attempt to construe God's grounding of the world in a non-mechanical way.

Then, Professor Corless avers that "Christianly we can say with Ruysbroeck that we can enter heaven only by leaving our intellects and emotions at its gates." To the contrary I would hold that Christianly what is said is that the intellect and the emotions *too* can be saved in every right sense of the word. The "Great Commandment" for Christians, rooted in the Jewish *shemā',* is that "you shall love the Lord your God with all your heart, mind, soul, strength" (Mark 12:28). The modes of love invoked here, clearly including emotional and intellectual, are not (*pace* Ruysbroeck) for mainstream Christian faith to be discarded at the threshold of the highest fulfillment but are—transfigured no doubt, but still analogically significant—to enter into the holiest of holies. Perhaps we encounter just one of the more salient sticking points in our overall Buddhist-Christian dialogue. However that may be, I find myself, as a would-be practitioner of Christian theology, compelled to dissent from an envisagement or symbolization of the ultimate that would disqualify from final communion with it any integral mode of the human spirit.

Professor Corless states: "If Mahayana Buddhism does nothing else in its dialogue with Christianity than clearly and repeatedly show that a reified God is a finite God and therefore not God, but an idol, it will have done well." Now on the one hand this statement raises problems for the process or dipolar theologian, or for the consciousness which process thought has sharpened in many of us, of the relative truth of the co-predicability of finitude, in some analogical sense at least, of the Divine. On the other hand, the statement could create the impression that Mahayana is, as it were, categorically the champion of what Tillich calls "the Protestant Principle"—the principle of God's unconditional transcendence of everything finite—whereas Christianity is chronically in need of having this truth brought home to it. The latter, I strongly agree, is true. Christianity does continuously need the reassertion of God's unconditionedness. Likewise we may agree with Professor Corless that this reassertion could or does beneficently come, in part, from Mahayana, as well as, I would think, from Theravada, from Hinduism, from Judaism, and perhaps especially from Islam. My point here would be that the "Protestant Principle"—the protest against idolatry—is manifested in most or all of the great traditions, certainly including Christianity itself, and is also *needed* within these traditions, including not least Mahayana Buddhism. I have in mind here, for example, the ostensible reification of divine power(s) in the Pure Land schools. Thus, I would widen Professor Corless' point. Yes, Mahayana will do well to call Christianity to account on the danger of idolatry; but also, vice versa, it will do well to hear Christian critique on the same end. And both traditions, in addition, may have constructive insights to share regarding the dipolar co-predicability of divine finitude that, in both, stands in dialectical tension with the unconditionedness of the ultimate.

There seems to be an ambiguity in Professor Corless' envisagement of the relation between the ultimate implicate order (the Ineffable Superconsciousness) and the manifest world. Following Bohm, Corless appears to maintain the unimpaired coinherence or mutual immanence of the World Ground and the explicate world which stands out from the ground. This would be equivalent to the symmetrical cosmology of, for example, Hua-Yen Buddhism. On the other hand Corless, again citing Bohm, also affirms that each explicate ordering of the world is a creative projection "which unfolds into a sequence of moments . . . not completely derivable from what came earlier in this sequence or set of such sequences." This sounds like Whitehead, and suggests a cumulative cosmology that differs significantly from the symmetrical type. Whatever Bohm may have intended in this connection, one gets the impression that Professor Corless may be positing an ontological freedom which could yield a real split between the Divine Ground and the world. Were he doing this it would in my judgment be quite biblical and Christian in that it would provide the basis for sin, or for that split between essence and existence that Tillich calls the backbone of Christian theology. I agree with Tillich that the ontological possibility and experienced actuality of such a split (i.e., of sin) is central to the Christian perspective. On the other hand, it seems definitely excluded by the Buddhist coinherence of nirvana and samsara. The latter coinherence is indeed paralleled by the Christian paradox of *simul justus et peccator,* but the specific Christian sense of this paradox depends upon there being the real split of sin which is amazingly overcome by God's grace. Professor Corless freely acknowledges that Buddhism and Christianity are in some ways concretely incompatible, but the point here is that they appear incompatible precisely in the envisaged relationship between the Divine Ground (or Unground) and the world, where Professor Corless, if I understand him, wants to suggest they are parallel or analogous. I would urge him to speak further to this matter of the freedom of the world to deviate from the Divine or (might we say?) the freedom of samsara to deviate from nirvana.

Finally, I am curious as to how far Professor Corless might extend his principle of the relatively autonomous coinherence of religious symbol systems, or of their ontological correlates in the structure of Being. In, through and beyond the penultimate structures which religions symbolize in such notions as Trinity and Emptiness, Corless posits an ineffable Superconsciousness, which nevertheless may be experienced in *satori,* presumably via a Christian as well as a Buddhist path. One recalls that Sri Ramakrishna claimed to experience *moksha* not only through the two religions named but also through a Hindu and a Muslim path. I wonder whether Professor Corless would construe *all* God-concepts or *all* ultimate notions—that is, the symbol systems of all religions—as equally legitimate explications of one and the same ineffable implicate order. I doubt that he would. But if not, what delimiting criteria would he use to exclude, perhaps, the neo-Aryan religion, or that of Jonestown, or whatever? Any such exclusion would require, would it not, as already mentioned, positing the possibility of sin and thus seemingly qualifying the coinherence of nirvana and samsara—at least in the case of excluded religions? Professor Corless does in fact seem to mention a criterion, at least implicitly, in his reference to an implicate order which explicates as basically supportive and loving. He says Buddhism and Christianity both presuppose such an implicative order. This seems clear in the Christian case because the Triune God can, indeed, will, as is historically manifest in Christ. But "can Emptiness will"? Or love? Gautama and the bodhisattvas can, of course. But can Emptiness? I wish Professor Corless had expounded this further. At one point deeply into the essay, his title question seems to be laid to rest by an appeal to apophatic experience. Yet it resurrects again at the very end of the essay. Can Emptiness will or love? As much as I enjoyed the essay, I did not experience the *satori* that Professor Corless says will dissolve the question. With regard to this particular question, like the doctors and saints of Omar Khayyam, who heard great argument, about it we seem to come out—albeit greatly enriched—by the same door wherein we went.

Bibliographical References

Abe, Masao

1963   "Buddhism and Christianity as a Problem of To-day: A Methodological Consideration," *Japanese Religions* 3:2 (11–22).
1968   "Christianity and Buddhism: Centering around Silence and Nihilism," *Japanese Religions* 5:3 (36–62).
1985   *Zen and Western Thought.* Hawaii.

Bohm, David

1981   *Wholeness and the Implicate Order.* Routledge.
1982 (1)   "The Enfolding-Unfolding Universe" in Wilber, 1982 (1).
1982 (2)   "Nature as Creativity," *ReVision* 5:2.

Bohm, David and Sheldrake, Rupert

1982   "Morphogenetic Fields and the Implicate Order," *ReVision* 5:2.

Bruteau, Beatrice

1983   "Insight and Manifestation: A Way of Prayer in a Christian Context," *Prabuddha Bharata,* 88.

Capra, Fritjof

1982 (1)   *The Turning Point.* Simon and Schuster.
1982 (2)   "*The Tao of Physics* Revisited," in Wilber, 1982 (1).

Carroll, Lewis

1963   *The Annotated Alice.* Introduction and notes by Martin Gardner. Cleveland, OH: World.

Cheng, Hsueh-Li (trans.)

1982   *Nagarjuna's "Twelve Gate Treatise."* Dordrecht: Reidel.

Conze, Edward

1957   *Buddhism.* Cassirer.
1962   *Buddhist Thought in India.* Allen and Unwin.

Corless, Roger

1979   "Sacred Text, Context and Proof-Text" in *The Critical Study of Sacred Texts,* ed. Wendy Doniger O'Flaherty. Berkeley Religious Studies, vol. 2.
1985   "Two Dramas of Spiritual Progress: The Lord and the Servant in Julian's *Showings* 51 and the Lost Heir in *Lotus Sutra* 4," *Mystics Quarterly* 11:2.
1986   "The Mutual Fulfillment of Buddhism and Christianity in Co-Inherent Superconsciousness" in *Buddhist-Christian Dialogue,* ed. Paul O. Ingram and Frederick J. Streng. Hawaii.

Dolan, John Patrick (ed.)

1962   *Unity and Reform: Selected Writings of Nicholas of Cusa.* Notre Dame.

Gilby, Thomas (ed.)

1955   *Saint Thomas Aquinas: Theological Texts.* Oxford.

Govinda, Lama Anagarika

1976   *Creative Meditation and Multi-Dimensional Consciousness.* Theosophical.

1977   *Foundations of Tibetan Mysticism.* Bombay: B.I. Publications.
1979   "The World View of a Mahayanan Buddhist," *ReVision* 2:2.
1981   *The Inner Structure of the I Ching.* San Francisco: Wheelwright.

Heidegger, Martin

1950   *Holzwege.* Frankfurt-am-Main.

Jackson, Kenneth Hurlstone (ed.)

1971   *A Celtic Miscellany.* Penguin.

Julian, Mother

1978   *A Book of Showings to the Anchoress Julian of Norwich,* ed. by Edmund College, O.S.A. and James Walsh, S.J. (2 vols.). Toronto: Pontifical Institute of Medieval Studies.

Kim, Hee-Jin

1980   *Dogen-Kigen—Mystical Realist.* Arizona.

Küng, Hans

1980 ET   *Does God Exist?* Doubleday. (Translated by Edward Quinn from *Existiert Gott?* Muenchen: Piper Verlag, 1978.)
n.d.   "Paradigm Change in Theology." Unpublished paper.

Kuhn, Thomas S.

1970   *The Structure of Scientific Revolutions.* Chicago, 2nd ed.

Kroy, Moshe

1982   "The Phenomenological Foundations of Transpersonal Psychology." Bombay: unpublished lecture.

Moltmann, Jürgen

1972   *Der gekreuzigte Gott.* Muenchen: Kaiser. (ET. by R.A. Wilson and John Bowden, *The Crucified God,* New York: Harper, 1974).

Murti, T.R.V.

1960   *The Central Philosophy of Buddhism.* Allen and Unwin.

Nietzsche, Friedrich

1909-1911   ET *Complete Works,* ed. Oscar Levy. 18 vols. New York.
1954-1956   *Werke in drei Baenden,* ed. Karl Schlechta. 3 vols. Munich: Carl Hanser.
1906   *Wille zur Macht (Taschenausgabe,* vol. 78). Leipzig: Kroener. (ET by Walter Kaufmann, *The Will to Power,* New York: Vintage Books, 1968)

Nishitani, Keiji

1982   *Religion and Nothingness.* California.

Ouspensky, Leonid and Lossky, Vladimir

1952   *The Meaning of Icons.* Boston Book and Art Shop.

Pelphrey, Brant

1982   *Love Was His Meaning: The Theology and Mysticism of Julian of Norwich.* Salzburg: Institut fuer Anglistik und Amerikanistik.

Rahner, Karl

1969   (ed.) *Sacramentum Mundi.* New York: Herder and Herder New York.
1978   *Foundations of Christian Faith.* Seabury.

Ramanan, K. Venkata

1978   *Nagarjuna's Philosophy.* Delhi: Banarsidass.

Sheldrake, Rupert

1981   *A New Science of Life.* Tarcher.

Stcherbatsky, Theodore

1978   *The Conception of Buddhist Nirvana.* Delhi: Banarsidass. (Originally Leningrad, 1927.)

Suzuki, Daisetz Teitaro

1979   *Mysticism: Christian and Buddhist.* Allen and Unwin.

Tillich, Paul

1969   *Der Mut zum Sein (Gesammelte Werke,* 11). Stuttgart: Evangelisches Verlagswerk. (Authorized German translation by Gertie Siemsen from *The Courage To Be,* New Haven CT: Yale University Press, 1952.)

Wilber, Ken

1980   "A Development Model of Consciousness" in *Beyond Ego,* ed. R.N. Walsh and F. Vaughan. Tarcher.

1982 (1)   (ed.) *The Holographic Paradigm and Other Paradoxes.* Shambhala.

1982   "Reflections on the New Age Paradigm" in Wilber 1982 (1).

Yokoi, Yuho

1976   *Zen Master Dogen.* Weatherhill.

Notes on the Contributors

MASAO ABE graduated from Kyoto University, Japan. He was Professor of Philosophy at Nara University of Education between 1952 and 1980 and has been a visiting professor at many universities in the United States. A student of Shin'ichi Hisamatsu, he is an exponent of the Kyoto School of Japanese Philosophy and a leading interpreter of Zen to the west. Between 1955 and 1957 he studied Christian theology at Union Theological Seminary in New York, and has recently become heavily involved in Buddhist-Christian Studies, especially by his public conversations with the process theologian John Cobb. His most recent book is *Zen and Western Thought* (University of Hawaii Press, 1985).

MICHAEL VON BRÜCK, Dr. theol. habil., Rostok University, 1980, is a German Lutheran pastor and a systematic theologian currently involved with the Buddhist-Christian Dialogue Research Project at the University of Tübingen. He taught for many years at Gurukul Lutheran Theological College in Madras, India, and has studied in Japan, and with Tibetan scholars. He has made important contributions to Hindu-Christian dialogue, especially in his book *Einheit der Wirklichkeit: Gott, Gottesfarhrung und Meditation im hinduistischen-christlichen Dialog* (München: Kaiser, 1987). Among his articles in English are "Zen Meditation for Christians" (*Gurukul Perspectives,* 22 [1982]), "Sunyata in Madhyamika Philosophy and the Christian Concept of God" (*Jeevadhara* [Kottayam], Nov. 1983, pp. 385–402) and "Advaita and Trinity" (*Indian Theological Studies,* 1983:1, pp. 37–60).

ROGER CORLESS studied theology at King's College, London (B.D., 1961) and Buddhism at the University of Wisconsin at Madison (Ph.D. 1973). He teaches in the Department of Religion at Duke University, Durham, North Carolina. His publications include books on Christian meditation and articles on Pure Land Buddhism and Buddhist-Christian Studies. He is a founding member of the Society for

Buddhist-Christian Studies, and currently its secretary. Having been baptized and confirmed in the Roman Catholic Church, and having taken refuge with a lama of the Tibetan Buddhist Gelugpa lineage, he is attempting to be a focus for both Buddhist and Christian practice, and to write out of that experience.

DURWOOD FOSTER is Professor of Christian Theology at the Pacific School of Religion and the Graduate Theological Union, Berkeley, California. He earned both his B.D. (1949) and Ph.D. (1956) at Union Theological Seminary, New York, and has taught there, at Duke University and at the University of Göttingen, Germany. He was Dean of the Pacific School of Religion between 1974 and 1979. An ordained minister of the United Methodist Church and a distinguished theologian, he is the author of many articles and of the book *The God Who Loves* (New York: Bruce, 1971).

PAUL INGRAM teaches religion at Pacific Lutheran University, Tacoma, Washington. He received his Th.M. (1964) and Ph.D. in History of Religions (1968) from Claremont Graduate School, and is a specialist in Japanese Buddhism, with particular emphasis on the Pure Land tradition. His most recent book is *A Study of Modern Buddhist-Christian Dialogue* (Edwin Mellen, 1987).

HANS KÜNG is one of the most distinguished living theologians in the Roman Catholic tradition, with numerous substantial publications to his credit. He earned his doctorate in theology from the Sorbonne in 1957 for work on Karl Barth, and has taught full and part time at many universities in Europe, the United Kingdom, Canada and the United States. Since 1980 he has been Professor of Ecumenical Theology and Director of the Institute for Ecumenical Research at the University of Tübingen.